Keon's Kitchen

By
Alan J. Boisvert

Secret Recipes from the Award-Winning Restaurant

Keon's 105 Bistro
105 Washington Street
Haverhill, MA 01832
978-521-0112
www.keons.com

Winner of the 2008 RAMAES award for
"Massachusetts' Restaurant of the Year"

ISBN   0-9821073-7-4
            978-0-9821073-7-9
February 2009

Published by Rybo's Publishing
105 Washington Street
Haverhill, MA 01832
978-521-0112
www.Keon's.com

Photography by Kevin Harkins, Harkins Photography, Londonderry, NH
www.harkinsphotography.com

Edited by Susan Smith, B.A., Bradford, MA

Book design and layout by IDT Design, robin@robinwrighton.com
Text set in Cronos , ITC Obelisk, ITC Tempus Sans.
Printed by King Printing Company, Inc., www.kingprinting.com

Published and printed in the United States of America

Dedication

To my wife, Lynn, whose inspiration and support gave me the confidence to pursue my dream. You have shown me that fairy tales can come true. You will always be my princess. I love you with all my heart.

To Sean and Nick, whose passion for cooking inspires me to continually challenge them. Their talent and enthusiasm are infectious.

To my siblings, Cindi, David, and Sandi, for all of their support over the years. I couldn't wish for a nicer, more loving family.

And, to Mom and Dad who always believed in me. I am the most fortunate man in the world to have you as both parents and friends.

Acknowledgments

To Rick Segel, you lit the flame of inspiration. The embers of my dream to write a cookbook have been smoldering in the back of my head for twenty years. It was you who ignited the fire. Your support and guidance have been invaluable to my quest.

My sincere thanks to Sean Demers, who works tirelessly to achieve perfection. Your devotion and passion will take you wherever you want to go in life.

Nick Gallo, who won't let a plate go through his hands that isn't perfect. Your dedication to your craft and commitment to excellence are commendable.

Robin Wrighton, my designer. For your enthusiasm and professionalism. Thank you for taking on this project. It has been a pleasure to work with you. I look forward to our next book!

Servers and friends: You have made Keon's a success. I'm just glad to be along for the ride! Tara Byrne, Stacey Condon, Jackie Cormier, Leanne Eastman, Janet Esposito, Nereyda Fernandez, Jen Fossarelli, Erin Kelleher, Sean Murphy, Sylvie Owens, Rudi Ramirez, Melissa Reynolds, Ashley Sigsworth, Beth Smith, Michelle Weitz…Go Time!!!

The Greater Haverhill Chamber of Commerce: Jim Jujuga, Leanne Eastman, Jen Cantwell, and the rest of the staff, for all that you do for the community of Haverhill and its citizens.

Kep Taylor, wherever you are! You encouraged me to pursue my dream and led me in the right direction. Never a day went by when you didn't make me laugh.

And to my wife, Lynn. Thank you for all of your help putting this book together. Without you, there would be no book!

Foreword

After judging and giving awards to businesses for the past 15 years, I know the elements that separate the winning businesses from those that come close, but don't quite make it. I look for exciting differences: from the way the service is delivered, to the way the product is presented. I look for attention to detail and those little enhancements that make an establishment special.

Keon's 105 Bistro is one of those special businesses that captures the customers at the door and holds their attention long after they have left. Businesses are built on word-of-mouth advertising; this is something every successful business understands. The problem many establishments have is they don't understand that if you want word-of-mouth advertising, you must give people something to talk about. Alan Boisvert is in the business of WOWing his customers every day and in every way, which gives them a lot to talk about.

"I knew this restaurant was special and an award winner when I first crossed the threshold!" That is why Keon's 105 Bistro in Haverhill, Massachusetts, won the RAMAE (Retailers Association of Massachusetts Award of Excellence) award for Restaurant of the Year in 2008 for the Commonwealth of Massachusetts. It is his philosophy, his passion, and his commitment to excellence that elevates Alan and his Bistro to that award-winning status. Lastly, this is a restaurant that has the panache of the finest restaurants in Chicago, New York, or San Francisco; yet it is located in a small, downtown setting in the suburbs of Boston. So I asked Alan the simplest and most basic question, "Why are you located in Haverhill, Massachusetts?" Alan's response was clear and to the point, "This is where I am from." ...... What a lucky break for Haverhill!

Rick Segel, Director and Founder of
The Retail Association Awards of Excellence Program

Contents

Contents

Introduction

My passion for cooking began when I was just 12 years old. I wanted to spend more time with my father, and the best way to do that was to go to work with him. He and Mom owned the Shawsheen Luncheonette in Andover, Massachusetts.

I began working Friday nights after school and Saturday mornings. Saturdays were tough. Up at 4am and not stopping until 2pm. We were always busy, it seemed. It was during that time Dad taught me the value of hard work and taking pride in what I do. My fondest childhood memories are those times spent in the luncheonette with Dad.

Mom loved to travel. I remember her saying, "Alan, go out and see the world. See it while you're young. There are so many wonderful places to see and to explore." Mom would describe the places she had been or wanted to see, and I would listen, intrigued.

Cooking was my ticket to travel. I quickly learned that the best hotels in the world are always looking for good, young talent. So, after graduating near the top of my class from the Culinary Institute of America in Hyde Park, New York, I applied to and landed a job at the Hotel Bayerischer Hof, in Munich, Germany. This was the first of 4, four-star/four diamond hotels in which I had the privilege of working.

I was able to get the job through an exchange program called Zihoga. They would secure work visas for the right applicants. Unfortunately, one of the criteria was you had to speak the language; if not fluently, pretty good at least. So, being young and cocky, I filled out the application, and in the space for language I just put down I spoke German fluently. I mean, how tough could it be to learn German if I was working there and everyone spoke the language anyway, right?

Well, needless to say, my first meeting with the executive chef didn't go over so well. He greeted me speaking German. It took about 30 seconds for him to figure out I had no idea what he was saying. I remember how the next couple of minutes went as if it were yesterday.

We were standing outside of his office with a bunch of cooks standing around all wanting to see this new cook, the American. When the chef realized I had no idea what he was saying, he stormed into his office and came out waving my application. The look on his face was not pretty, and I was picturing him calling security and having me thrown out of the hotel.

"Herr Boisvert, it say's here that you speak German fluently. It is clear to me that you do not," he said in a very stern voice. I'll admit, at this point I was quaking in my boots. A few smirks and whispers behind me didn't help the situation.

"How much German do you speak?" he asked.

"None," I said sheepishly. "But I'm willing to learn," I offered eagerly.

"Well, if you don't speak any German, why did you put on your application that you speak it fluently?" he asked, not at all happy.

"Because I wanted to work for you. I understand that you are one of the best chefs in Europe." I said, winging it as I went. "My chefs at the Culinary Institute, Chef Faulkner and Chef Hennin, speak very highly of you," I continued, completely full of crap. "Would you have hired me if I put on my application that I didn't speak any German?" I asked, at this point rambling on.

"No, of course not," he responded tersely.

"Well, I'm here, and I'm willing to learn as fast as I can," I said, not wanting to lose this opportunity. At this point he actually turned away, and I swear he chuckled a bit to himself.

In the end, he agreed to let me stay as long as I understood that English would not be spoken in the kitchen, and I would have to learn German in order to stay.

I ended up attending school Monday through Friday from 9am to noon to learn German while working every night until midnight or later, cooking in their signature restaurant, "The Grill Room."

A year and-a-half later, I was contacted by The Peabody Hotel in Memphis, Tennessee. I had interviewed with them while I was a student at the Culinary Institute. They had a position opening as the executive sous chef in one of their restaurants, "Dux".

Chef Ralph Bouton was a creative and energetic chef willing to teach his craft to anyone with the desire to learn.

The following year, I was asked to be part of their opening team for The Peabody Hotel in Orlando, Florida. Both Peabody Hotels are or were four star/four diamond properties and ranked in the top 50 in the world.

Three years as the banquet chef at the Marriott Long Wharf in Boston paved the way for a position at the Crescent Court in Dallas, another four star/four diamond hotel. There, I held positions of am sous chef, pm sous chef and banquet chef over a three and-a-half year stint.

As the years went by, hotel life took its toll. The long hours, working every holiday (hotels are never closed), and the late nights got to be a bit much. I decided there must be a way where I could experience the passion for the food industry without driving myself into the ground. Years later I found it, or more specifically, my wife, Lynn, found it in Keon's 105 Bistro.

Lynn encouraged me to buy Keon's, and although I was slow to follow through, her encouragement convinced me it was right for me. Lynn had the confidence that I could make a go of it. I wasn't about to let her down.

I wanted Keon's 105 Bistro to be that, a bistro. There are many definitions for bistro and even more interpretations. I am of the belief a bistro is a cozy, upscale eatery. Whether that is correct or not, I don't really care. That is what Keon's 105 Bistro is.

We make almost everything we serve, on property. A few exceptions do exist. For instance, we have a wonderful ice cream shop next door, England's Micro Creamery. They make the most flavorful ice creams you can imagine. Jane, the owner, has made cantaloupe ice cream, watermelon sorbet, and a white peach ice cream that will knock your socks off! When I can get a product of the quality she serves, I would be an idiot not to incorporate it into my menu.

We try not to over complicate our menu or use too many conflicting ingredients at Keon's. I feel too many chefs today want to impress their clientele by writing menus with lots of ingredients. They assume this will impress their guests when they see a menu with lots of exotic items. The truth is, simple is better. Each dish should have one ingredient that sets it apart. All other ingredients should compliment the item you are trying to focus on.

We try to blend flavors, textures, and colors on every plate. When something looks good, it generally tastes good. If the dish already has great flavors, and it is plated properly with a balance of color and texture, then it will taste even better in your guest's mind because of the presentation.

I like cooking with Kosher salt and coarse-ground, black pepper. The reasons are obvious to the trained professional. Kosher salt, when used properly, enhances food flavor without it tasting salty. Iodized salt always tastes salty. Coarse-ground black pepper also gives food a wonderful flavor. This, I'll admit, may be a personal preference, but try it. You won't be disappointed.

The recipes in this book are, at times, time consuming. The actual prep time may not take long, but the cook times may. This is because I like to slow cook meats and use reduction sauces at my restaurant. Reduction sauces are classical sauces with a bit of a twist. They are thickened by reduction instead of adding a starch. I believe in simmering stock longer than traditional recipes call for. I find that I get more flavor simmering a stock for 8 hours than 4 hours. Roasting tomatoes for a tomato sauce for 6 hours, as opposed to stovetop cooking, is another example of how we like to do things at Keon's.

When using the recipes in this book, be sure to read through them first and understand the procedure before beginning. Some of the recipes may have three things going at once, and timing is of great importance when executing. Our Three Brothers dish is a prime example.

I have listed the ingredients in all of my recipes in the order they will be used in the dish. This will make it easier for you to execute without getting confused.

My current chefs, Nick Gallo and Sean Demers, share the same passion for food that I do. Their willingness to do the job right and not take shortcuts are what makes them such talented chefs. Their pride in what they put out is evident in every plate they produce. Many of the recipes in this book have been developed or tweaked by them. So, I hope you enjoy the book and recipes contained within.

Hints and Tips for Cooking

If you want to prepare wonderful dishes for your guests, it is important to keep the basics of cooking in mind. By the "basics", I mean: proper seasoning, cooking techniques, and plating. Even the best recipes will turn out to be less than desirable if short cuts are taken during the cooking/plating process.

1. Follow the recipe

If a recipe calls for cream, use cream. Do not substitute milk and expect the same results.

If it calls for butter, do not substitute margarine, etc.

Fresh herbs should be used whenever called for as dried herbs are stronger in flavor. They do not taste the same as fresh herbs.

2. Adhere to proper cooking techniques

This is very important! When sautéing, for example, the pan should be heated to a very high temperature before adding the oil. This opens the pores in the metal, and it allows the oil to fill those pores preventing your proteins from sticking.

Having a hot pan and very hot oil will caramelize the natural sugars in the product, giving it a nice even color. Never put your food into a cold pan thinking it will speed the cooking process. It won't. It will, however, stick and ruin whatever it is that you were cooking.

3. Season your food

Proper seasoning makes good food great. If you want to impress your guests, then proper seasoning is a good place to start.

I like to use kosher salt instead of iodized salt because it tastes less salty. Yes, less salty! I know it sounds weird, but try it yourself. Put a little of each on your fingertip and taste it. You will see what I mean.

When using black pepper, I prefer a coarse grind. Again, the flavor, I feel, is much better than table grind pepper. Even salads need a pinch of seasoning to bring out the flavors within.

4. Blend colors and textures

The key to a great dish is how it looks to your guest when they first see it. Having various colors, textures, and height will give your food eye appeal. Remember, if it looks good, it probably will taste good.

I like to have various texture on all of my plates. For example, our Chilean Sea Bass is served with Smoked Ham Risotto and Root Vegetable Chips. The firmness of the sea bass is complimented by the creamy risotto and the crispy root vegetable chips giving the dish a nice balance of texture and color.

I don't recommend serving grilled meat with grilled vegetables and grilled potatoes, as everything on the plate will have the same char flavor and dark colors.

5. Don't forget the basics

By this I mean, when sautéing, be sure that the item has a nice sear to it before turning it over in the pan.

When braising, be sure to properly brown all sides of the meat to give it a better look and flavor before adding the liquid to the pot.

When baking, be sure the oven is up to temperature before adding your product.

Do not stand with the oven door open to check if your product is done. When checking for doneness of a product in the oven, remove it from the oven, close the door, check your product, and return it to the oven.

I often see people check the temperature of a roast by opening the door and putting the thermometer in the roast, they wait a minute to get a reading and then close the door. When this is done, 200 or more degrees of oven heat will be lost. This will throw off your cooking time when roasting. When baking, it can ruin a product.

When blanching vegetables, be sure to have a container of ice water available and ready for shocking. This will give vegetables a vibrant color and stop the cooking process, preventing over-cooked product.

6. Allow your proteins to rest before serving

Letting proteins that have just been cooked to rest for 5-10 minutes before serving will relax the muscles and prevent the juices from escaping. This keeps your food juicy and tasty.

Have you eaten a steak right off the grill and when you were done noticed a pool of liquid on your plate? That moisture should have been in the steak! The same goes for poultry.

7. Timing is everything

Read your recipe first and determine if there are multiple steps. If so, be sure to time them accordingly.

For example, for the Three Brothers dish, I recommend the Whipped Yukon Potatoes are already finished and holding before sautéing the proteins. The haricots vert (green beans) should already be blanched as well and only need to be heated in butter at the time of service. This ensures that all of my food is hot at plating time.

8. Clean as you go

This has nothing to do with executing good food, but will prevent you from hours of cleaning afterwards. Pots and pans are much easier to clean when the food has just come out of them. A skillet can be cleaned in seconds if it is rinsed while still hot. This will prevent that overwhelmed feeling of having to clean the kitchen after a wonderful meal.

Measurements

Pinch	=	1/8 teaspoon	64 ounces	=	½ gallon
3 teaspoons	=	Tablespoon	128 ounces	=	1 gallon
2 tablespoons	=	1 ounce	2 cups	=	1 pint
2 ounces	=	¼ cup	2 pints	=	1 quart
8 ounces	=	1 cup	2 quarts	=	½ gallon
16 ounces	=	1 pint	4 quarts	=	1 gallon
32 ounces	=	1 quart			

Cooking Temperature Guide

The temperatures refer to the center of the meat after cooking. When using a meat thermometer, try as best you can to have the tip of the meat thermometer as close to the center of the protein you are temping.

Rare	=	120 degrees
Med/Rare	=	130 degrees
Medium	=	140 degrees
Medium/Well	=	150 degrees
Well Done	=	160 degrees

Tools of The Trade

These are some of the kitchen tools that will make your life in the kitchen a little easier:

- blender
- candy thermometer or a deep fat thermometer
- coffee grinder – use this to grind your peppercorns
- food processor
- immersible blender – found at most kitchen stores
- 8″ skillet
- 10″ skillet
- 12″ skillet
- 8-quart stock pot – tall, for stocks, soups, and sauces
- 8-quart rondo – this is a wide pot that is shallow, used for braising
- 8″ chef's knife

- boning knife
- paring knife
- mandolin – this is used for slicing and jullienned vegetables
- measuring spoons
- measuring cups
- meat thermometer
- slotted spoons
- spatulas
- squirt bottles – for garnishing plates with sauces in streaks
- tongs
- vegetable peelers
- whisks – small and medium-sized
- wooden spoons – small and medium-sized

HINTS AND TIPS FOR COOKING

Recipes By Course

Sauces, Dressings and Chutneys

Appetizers

Soups & Salads

Raviolis

Stocks

Main Courses

Side Dishes

Desserts

Sauces, Dressings, and Chutneys

Sauces, dressings, and chutneys are the ingredients that make your appetizers, salads, and main courses taste great. If you are reading this book, then I assume you plan on WOWing your guests. That means you want to take pride in every aspect of the meal. Taking the time to make a great looking salad, and then plopping down a bottled dressing, doesn't do it for me. Don't get me wrong; there are some commercial dressings out there that are very good, but they are not yours!

When you make your own dressing or sauce, you have the power to change it to your liking. I have given you some basic dressings and sauces. Make the recipes I have given you first, and then get creative. Try adding a fresh herb like rosemary to the Honey-Champagne Vinaigrette. You could add a little thyme or sage to the Keon's Supreme Sauce. The options are endless.

Whenever you are going to change a recipe, be sure that you have tasted it the way it was designed before making the change. This will increase the chance of success. Remember, when making the changes, do it in small amounts first. Don't add an ingredient in a large amount because you like the flavor on its own. I assure you, you won't be happy with the end result.

Chutneys are fun to make and enjoyable to eat. They are said to have originated in India.

The definition of a chutney is, "A pungent relish made of fruit, spices, and herbs." As you can see, there are no ingredients in the definition. The options, therefore, are endless. I have given you 3 recipes I feel will compliment as many dishes as you can think of. Enjoy!

Aioli

An Aioli is nothing more than a homemade garlic mayonnaise. It is said that aioli comes from the Provence region of France. It is used as an accompaniment or a dipping sauce. It is also used as a sauce for pastas, poultry and fish.

If you wish, substitute the blended olive oil for a good quality extra virgin olive oil. This will give you a much stronger flavor.

4 ea	fresh garlic cloves
4 ea	egg yolks
2 T	lemon juice
2 T	dijon mustard
3 ½ cups	blended olive oil (80/20 is a good mix)
¾ tsp	kosher salt
½ tsp	black pepper, coarse grind

Yield: 4 ½ cups

Place the garlic cloves in a food processor or blender and mince—or you can do it by hand. Add the egg and process briefly. Add the dijon mustard. With the processor on a low speed, very slowly pour in half of the olive oil. Add the lemon juice, and then slowly pour in the remaining olive oil. Process just until the mixture thickens and emulsifies. Season with salt and pepper.

Red Pepper Aioli

| ¼ cup | roasted red peppers, puréed smooth |

This is great for potato salad, macaroni salad, or egg salad. When using this recipe for these salads, do not use extra virgin oil in the original recipe; instead, substitute canola oil.

Place the roasted peppers in the food processor with the garlic, and proceed with the Aioli recipe as instructed.

Basil Aioli

| ½ cup | fresh basil |
| 1/3 cup | olive oil |

Make the Aioli recipe as instructed.

Place the basil and 1/3 cup olive oil in a food processor and blend until smooth. Whisk this slowly into the basic recipe.

Lemon Aioli

Follow the Aioli recipe, but double the lemon juice, and add ¼ teaspoon of fresh lemon rind.

Peppercorn Dressing

Follow the Aioli recipe, and add 1 ½ tsp of coarse grind black pepper, ½ cup grated parmesan cheese, and 1/3 cup light cream.

Apple Chutney

This is a great condiment for pork chops, turkey sandwiches, grilled swordfish, halibut, or chicken.

Make the recipe and store it in the refrigerator for up to 3 weeks. The flavors get better over the first few days.

1 T	unsalted butter
½ cup	red onions, small diced
3 ea	large granny smith apples, peeled and cored, 1" diced
½ cup	dark raisins
1 oz	cold water
1 T	lemon juice
¼ cup	red wine vinegar
¼ cup	brown sugar
1 tsp	orange rind
1 tsp	fresh minced ginger
¼ tsp	allspice
½ tsp	turmeric
¼ tsp	kosher salt

Yield: 4 cups

Melt the butter in a medium-sized saucepan over medium heat. Add the red onions, and sauté until translucent. Add the apples and raisins, and sauté an additional 3 minutes. Add the rest of the ingredients and bring to a simmer. Reduce the heat to low, and allow it to simmer for 45 minutes, stirring occasionally. Chill before serving.

Balsamic Dressing

This dressing is an emulsified dressing. It makes a great dressing for salads and grilled vegetables. When brushed lightly on grilled meats and fish, it blends nicely with the char flavor. This recipe can also be used as a marinade, but I suggest you be careful not to use it too heavy. Lightly coat the protein to be marinated, and do not let it marinate for more than a few hours.

½ cup	balsamic vinegar
3 T	dijon mustard
2 T	sugar
½ packet	Good Seasons Italian Dressing® dry mix
1 T	garlic, minced
¼ tsp	black pepper, coarse grind
¼ tsp	kosher salt
2 cups	blended oil

Yield: Approximately 3½ cups

In a food processor, place all ingredients except for the oil. Blend for 15 seconds. In a slow stream, add the oil until it is emulsified.

Blood Orange Vinaigrette

This dressing is good on a number of green salads, including arrugala, spinach, frisée, etc. You can use either canola oil or extra virgin olive oil, depending on how strong of a blood orange flavor you want. When using olive oil, it will dominate the blood orange flavor. Some chefs find this is the desired taste; others do not. I go back and forth with this decision, depending on what it is that I am dressing.

I recommend you make this recipe twice, once with each oil. Then you can decide for yourself.

½ cup	blood orange juice (approx. 2 blood oranges)
½ tsp	blood orange rind
½ tsp	granulated sugar
3 T	champagne vinegar or white wine vinegar
1 T	shallot, diced fine
1 tsp	chopped chives
¼ tsp	kosher salt
pinch	black pepper, coarse grind
½ cup	canola oil or olive oil

Yield: 1 cup

Combine all of the ingredients (except the oil) in a medium-sized bowl. Slowly whisk in the oil in a steady stream to emulsify. If you are making this in advance, you will need to re-whisk it before serving as this will not hold together for long periods of time.

Brown Butter Sauce

Brown butter is exactly what it sounds like–butter that has been browned in a pan. When butter is browned, it takes on a nutty flavor and enhances, in my opinion, anything it touches.

When browning butter, the key is to have a pan that is hot, but not smoking hot. Put your butter in, and watch it brown; remove from the heat, and nape' over whatever dish you are saucing.

Options:

Once the butter is browned, you can add many different herbs to enhance various dishes. Fresh sage, rosemary, and thyme are a few of my favorites. Each one has a unique flavor. However, I do not recommend combining herbs.

The trick to extract the most and best flavor is to add the herbs as soon as the butter has browned and to swirl in the pan quickly before saucing your dish.

Keon's Caesar Dressing

This is an emulsified dressing. I like my Caesar dressing thick because when mixing it with lettuce that has been washed, it will be diluted.

Again, like many of my sauces and dressings, there are more uses than I have written. This makes a great spread on grilled chicken sandwiches, burgers, and turkey burgers. It also works well on proteins that are to be grilled. Brush it on lightly an hour or so before grilling, and taste the flavor it adds to chicken, beef, and oily fish, such as bluefish, salmon and even swordfish.

5 ea	anchovies
6 ea	cloves of garlic
3 T	dijon mustard
2 T	Worcestershire Sauce®
¼ cup	lemon juice
1 oz	red wine vinegar
3 ea	egg yolks
1 tsp	black pepper, coarse grind
¼ tsp	kosher salt
¾ cup	parmesan cheese, grated
2 cups	olive oil, not extra virgin

Yield: Approximately 4 ½ cups

Put the first 9 ingredients In a food processor and blend until smooth. Add the parmesan cheese and blend. Add the oil in a slow stream and blend until all the oil has been incorporated.

This should be a thick dressing, the consistency of mayonnaise!

Check seasoning. Add salt and pepper if necessary.

Baked Diver Scallops
with Butternut Cream

Page 64

This scallop appetizer can also be served as an entrée. It goes well with an herbed risotto, wild rice, basmati rice or any variety of fresh vegetables.

Korean BBQ Pork with homemade Yukon Potato Chips and Aioli

Page 160

This dish has wonderful versatility. It makes a great appetizer, as shown, or a superb sandwich when served on a fresh bulkie roll or focaccia bread.

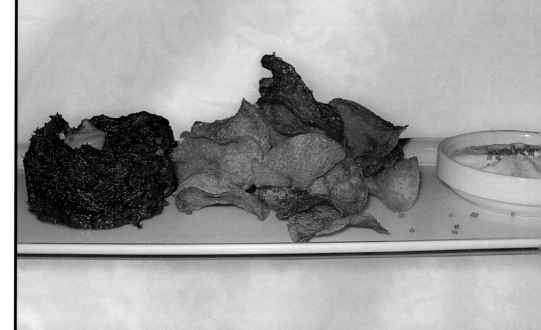

Romano Chicken Fingers
with Sun Dried Tomato Risotto

Page 78

This is one of the very popular appetizers we have at Keon's. It combines textures, flavors and color. Whenever you can accomplish that, the dish has a greater chance of success.

Texas Crab Cakes

Page 82

Some restaurants serve their crab cakes fried, some serve theirs pan seared or sautéed. I like to pan sear ours in a very hot pan in a thin layer of oil. I find they are never greasy and always maintain that high level of quality. I cannot emphasize enough the importance of serving only the best. Use only *fresh*, lump crabmeat.

Tomato-Mozzarella Salad

Page 107

The key to a good Tomato-Mozzarella Salad is the ingredients. I only use vine-ripened tomatoes. They always have a deeper, richer flavor and a deep red color to them.

Keon's Caesar Dressing

Page 32

This is an emulsified dressing. I like my Caesar dressing thick, because when mixing it with lettuce that has been washed, it will be diluted.

This makes a great spread on grilled chicken sandwiches, burgers, and turkey burgers. It also works well on proteins to be grilled. Brush it on lightly an hour or so before grilling, and taste the flavor it adds to chicken, beef, and oily fish, such as bluefish, salmon and even swordfish.

Keon's Caesar Salad

Page 103

A classic Caesar salad is romaine, Caesar Dressing, croutons, and anchovies. Since the majority of our customers are not fond of anchovies sitting on top of their salad, we only use them in the dressing.

I want some substance and color in my salad. For this reason, I add Marinated Cherry Tomatoes. You can also add roasted red peppers, shaved red onions, kalamata olives. Try thinking outside the box, your guests will be pleased.

Honey-Champagne Vinaigrette

Page 55

This, like many of our recipes at Keon's, has more than one application. It is our standard dressing for our Bibb Salad. It can also be used as a marinade for meats, fish, and poultry.

Bibb Salad

Page 102

This nice, light salad is a perfect start to a meal. Bibb lettuce, also known as Boston lettuce, is very mellow in flavor. Its leaves are soft and pleasing to the palate. Be careful not to overdress a salad using bib lettuce, as it will absorb the dressing quickly and become soggy.

Adding roasted red and/or yellow peppers will give this plate more color. The Spiced Pecans add crunch and flavor.

Properly Caramelized Vegetables for Stock

Veal Stock Recipe Found on Page 144

The key to making a very good Veal Stock is in the caramelizing of the vegetables and bones. The darker you get the vegetables and bones without burning them, the richer and stronger your stock will come out.

Don't take short cuts. Take your time, the end result will be well worth it.

Stocks and Broths

Page 144

Remember, always allow your stocks to simmer for the recommended time specified in the recipe. Periodically, brush the inside of the pot above the liquid to prevent a crust from forming. This crust has great flavor that you will be losing if you allow it to adhere to the inside of the pot.

French Onion Soup

Page 96

For a really good onion soup, the onions must be caramelized properly. This takes an hour or more. Proper caramelizing of the onions will give your soup a deep rich color and flavor. Do not rush the caramelizing process.

Spinach and Arrugala Salad with Warm Cider Dressing

Page 106

This salad is a great winter salad, although, I enjoy it year-round. The cider dressing should be warm, not boiling. The idea is to slightly wilt the greens. This way, once it hits the cold greens, is plated, and served, your guests will enjoy something that is just warmer than room temperature.

Pan Seared Diver Scallops with Arrugala and Golden Raisin Chutney

Page 168

This is a great cold weather dish. It combines the savory flavor of the arrugala and the sweet flavors of the chutney. I put this on the menu over a year ago and cannot take it off. Although, I feel that this is a perfect cold weather dish, our customers love it year-round.

Grilled Corn and Potato Fritters

Page 69

There are many uses for grilled corn. It can be used in fillings for raviolis; used in stuffings for meat, poultry, pork and lamb; with peppers, cilantro and black beans for salsa; and as a garnish to salads. The uses are endless, and the flavor it adds is spectacular! Recipes are included in this book. These are also wonderful when drizzled with honey!

Cider Glazed Pork Chops

Page 148

This has been a staple at Keon's since the previous owner, Michael Keon, opened its doors in the late 1990's.

Cipollini Onion Gravy

This gravy goes well with steaks, roasts, sirloin tips, tenderloin tips, and even on a roast beef sandwich. It is rich with flavor and easy to make. Typically, a gravy is made with pan juices. You can add the juices of any meat you are cooking to this recipe if there are any. This has the look of a gravy, and that is why I call it one.

2 T	butter, unsalted
1 cup	cipollini onion, peeled, sliced thin
1 tsp	flour
1 tsp	dijon mustard
¼ tsp	kosher salt
¼ tsp	black pepper, coarse grind
1 cup	Demi Glace (page 62)
¼ cup	heavy cream

Yield: 6 portions

Melt the butter in a small saucepot over medium-high heat. Add the sliced cipollini onions, and sauté until they are golden brown. Stir in the flour until smooth. Add the dijon, Demi Glace, salt and pepper. If you have juices from a roast or pan drippings from the item you are serving this with, add them now. Do not add more than ¼ cup. Bring the sauce to a boil, and whisk in the cream. Bring back to a boil, and remove from the heat.

Citrus Vinaigrette

This is a dressing that I tend to use more as a marinade than a dressing. It gives shrimp an awesome flavor while tenderizing them. This also works well as a marinade for scallops, swordfish, and chicken as well. Enjoy!

2 T	lemon juice, fresh
2 T	lime juice, fresh
1/3 cup	orange juice, fresh
1 tsp	dijon mustard
1 tsp	honey
1/4 cup	red onions, fine diced
1 tsp	fresh dill, chopped
1/2 tsp	kosher salt
1/2 tsp	black pepper, coarse grind
1 cup	extra virgin olive oil

Yield: 2 cups

In a medium-sized bowl, whisk together all of the ingredients except the olive oil. Then slowly drizzle in the oil in a slow stream while whisking.

Check seasoning.

Fra Diavolo Sauce

This spicy tomato sauce has many uses. It goes great with lobster, pastas, chicken and a variety of fish.

The prep time is quick, but the cook time is 3-4 hours for the best results.

3 T	olive oil
2 T	garlic, chopped
½ cup	red wine
2 ea	24 oz cans of whole plum tomatoes
1 ½ tsp	kosher salt
1 tsp	red pepper flakes
¾ tsp	black pepper, coarse grind
2 T	pesto, store-bought is fine

Yield: Approximately 1 ½ quarts

Heat the oil in a 4-quart saucepot. Add the garlic, and stir until translucent. DO NOT BROWN. Add the red wine, and reduce until the wine is almost evaporated. Add the rest of the ingredients and bring to a boil. Place the pot in a 350-degree oven, and cook for two hours*. Remove from the oven, close the door, and stir. If the sauce appears to be too dry, add 1 cup of chicken broth, stock, or water. Stir again and return to the oven for 1 hour longer. Remove from the oven and purée using a hand held immersible blender.

Check seasoning.

* Be sure that your pot has handles that are oven safe!

Golden Raisin Chutney

A chutney, in the classical sense, is a sauce or condiment that combines sweet and savory flavors. This does that as well as any I've had. This is the ingredient, in my opinion, that makes our scallop dish so good. It blends the sweetness of the golden raisins with the savory flavors of dijon mustard and apple smoked bacon.

This can be used as a condiment on burgers, steaks, chicken, and any hearty seafood, such as scallops, swordfish, halibut, and sea bass.

1 lb	apple smoked bacon, cut into ¼" strips-crosswise (1/4" x 1")
1 doz	cipollini onions, peeled and cut into 1/8 pie wedges
1 ea	celery stalk, small dice
1 tsp	fresh garlic, minced
¾ cup	golden raisins
1 T	butter
¼ tsp	ground cinnamon
2 T	dijon mustard
¼ cup	Cider Reduction (page 60)
TT	kosher salt
TT	black pepper, coarse grind

Yield: Approximately 4 cups

Render the strips of bacon in a pan over medium heat until crispy. Remove the bacon, and save for later. Add the cipollini onions and the diced celery to the bacon fat. Cook for about 20 minutes over medium-high heat or until the onions are beginning to caramelize. Drain ½ of the bacon fat, and add the garlic stirring constantly for 1 minute over medium heat. Add the rest of the ingredients, and reduce to low heat. Stir occasionally. Cook for 20 minutes. Keep warm until service.

Hollandaise Sauce

I love hollandaise sauce for many reasons. The flavor, color, and texture seems to compliment everything it touches. My favorite is Tomato-Basil Hollandaise, which can be used to compliment fish, meats, poultry, eggs, and even vegetables.

Hollandaise is one of the five classic mother sauces in French cuisine. A mother sauce is a sauce that all other sauces are derived from. Hollandaise is an emulsified sauce, meaning that fat cells are suspended in liquid. Mayonnaise and creamy dressings are other examples of emulsified sauces.

I'm going to give you the recipe for a basic hollandaise and a few variations. Once you have mastered the art of making a hollandaise, the variations are endless. You can add fresh herbs, citrus juices, vegetable purées, fruit purées, etc.

³/₄ cup	unsalted butter, melted
4 ea	egg yolks
1 ½ T	lemon juice
¼ tsp	kosher salt
1/8 tsp	cayenne pepper
2 T	hot water

Yield: 1 ½ cups

Heat the butter in a small saucepan until hot and foamy. In a medium-sized bowl, combine the eggs with the hot water while whisking vigorously. Add the lemon juice, salt, and cayenne while still whisking. Continue to whisk and drizzle in the hot butter slowly. If you add the butter too quickly, the sauce will break. By this, I mean that the eggs and butter will separate. When a hollandaise sauce has broken, it is difficult, though not impossible, to bring it back. It would be better to start over.

Once all the butter has been incorporated, place the bowl over very low heat and continue to whisk until the sauce has thickened. This should only take 1 minute or so. Be careful not to scramble the eggs! Hollandaise should be served right away or within a ½ hour or so.

Tomato-Basil Hollandaise

| 1 T | tomato paste |
| 1 T | fresh basil, chopped |

Add the tomato paste to the egg yolks and hot water while following the above recipe. Stir in the basil just before serving.

Blood Orange Hollandaise

This is a great sauce for halibut, haddock, sea bass, shrimp and any other seafood you can imagine. It also compliments vegetables such as broccoli, asparagus, white asparagus, and cauliflower.

Substitute 3 T of blood orange juice or purée for the lemon juice, and follow the hollandaise sauce recipe.

Citrus Hollandaise

Another good variation for of all kinds of seafood. Follow the main recipe and add ½ tsp each of lime and orange zest.

Béarnaise Sauce

This is another classic French sauce usually served with filet mignon or steak of some kind.

1 T	fresh chopped tarragon
2 T	white wine vinegar
2 T	white wine
2 T	shallots, chopped fine

Combine all ingredients, and cook over low heat until the liquid is evaporated. Cool and stir into the basic hollandaise sauce.

Honey-Champagne Vinaigrette

This, like many of our recipes at Keon's, has more than one application. It is our standard dressing for our Bibb Salad. It can also be used as a marinade for meats, fish, and poultry. This is one of the few recipes that we actually use ingredients that are a commercial mix. The Good Seasons® brand is consistent and flavorful.

1 cup	champagne vinegar
2 T	dijon mustard
¾ cup	honey
1 T	Good Seasons® Italian Dressing dry mix
¼ tsp	kosher salt
¼ tsp	black pepper, coarse grind
1 pint	oil, vegetable
¼ cup	chives, chopped

Yield: 1 quart

Place the vinegar, mustard, honey, Good Seasons®, salt, and pepper in a food processor. Blend. While the processor is running, slowly add the oil in a steady stream. When all of the oil is incorporated, shut off the machine. Stir in chives.

Keon's Supreme Sauce

Okay, this one has great flavor, just don't tell your cardiologist you are eating it three times per week. This is the sauce we use on our Three Brothers dish at Keon's. It has been a winner since we opened the doors in the fall of 2005. I suspect it will continue to be a winner for a long time to come.

2 T	butter, unsalted
2 ea	shallots, minced
1 ea	garlic cloves
¼ cup	white wine
½ cup	lemon juice
2 pt	Roasted Chicken Stock (page 143)
1 pt.	heavy cream
2 T	chopped basil
1 tsp	kosher salt
½ tsp	black pepper, coarse grind

*Uncooked Roux

1 oz	butter, softened
1 T	flour

Yield: Aproximately 7 cups

Mix the flour and the butter into a smooth paste.

In a small saucepot, melt the butter over medium heat. Add the shallots and garlic and stir constantly until translucent. Add the wine and lemon juice and reduce until a thin layer coats the bottom of the pot. Add the Roasted Chicken Stock, and reduce by half. Add the cream, bring to a boil, and reduce it to a simmer. Add the uncooked roux* while whisking vigorously. Remove from the heat and whisk until thick. Stir in fresh chopped basil. Season to taste.

Pico di Gallo Mayo

This stuff is awesome! We serve it with our crab cakes, and our customers love it. If you are not very fond of heat, then only use ½ of a jalapeño for this recipe. If you like heat, then use 2.

This is a great base for potato salad, macaroni salad, egg salad. If you thin it out with a bit of half-and-half and rice wine vinegar, it makes a great salad dressing. The options are endless.

In the recipe I call for extra heavy mayonnaise. This is a thick mayonnaise. Do not use a mayo dressing, which would have a thin consistency.

2 T	red onion, small dice
2 T	red peppers, small dice
2 T	green peppers, small dice
1 ea	jalapeños
2 T	cilantro, chopped
2 T	lime juice
1 cup	extra heavy mayo
1 tsp	Old Bay® Seasoning
¼ tsp	cayenne pepper
TT	kosher salt
TT	black pepper, coarse grind

Yield: 1 ½ cups

Mix all ingredients and let stand in refrigerator for 1 hour.

Sweet Corn-Serrano Sauce

One of my favorite all time sauces. Once you have made this and tasted it, you will know why. This makes a great sauce for shrimp, pasta, poultry, white fish, pork, and veal.

2 T	butter, unsalted
¼ cup	yellow onion, small dice
1 ea	yellow peppers, small dice
1–2 ea	Serrano chili peppers, depending on how hot you like it
½ tsp	garlic, fresh chopped
¼ tsp	cumin
1 qt	Roasted Chicken Stock (page 143)
1 cup	fresh corn, removed from the cob (frozen, if desired)
1 oz	butter, softened
1 oz	flour
1 cup	heavy cream
1 tsp	kosher salt
½ tsp	black pepper, coarse grind

Yield: Approximately 1 ½ qts

Melt the butter in a 3-quart saucepot over medium-high heat. Add the onions and peppers, and sweat the vegetables for about 3 minutes, stirring occasionally. Add the garlic and cumin, and stir for 1 minute, do not brown! Add the Roasted Chicken Stock and the corn. Bring to a boil, and then reduce to a simmer for 30 minutes. Remove from the heat and blend in a blender until smooth. *Be careful blending hot liquids!*

Strain through a mesh strainer, and return to medium heat.

In a bowl, blend the softened butter and flour until smooth. Add this to the simmering sauce while whisking vigorously. Whisk until smooth. Add the cream, and bring it to a simmer. Season with salt and pepper.

Pink Pomodoro Sauce

Pink pomodoro sauce is one that combines the richness of alfredo sauce with the tanginess of tomato sauce. I like to use a roasted tomato sauce for this application. But, to make things a bit easier for you, we will be using your favorite store-bought sauce. This is the sauce for our romano chicken fingers at Keon's. It is also great with pastas, raviolis, chicken, lasagna, seafood and, meats.

2 T	olive oil
1 T	garlic, peeled, chopped
1 cup	heavy cream
1 T	corn starch
2 oz.	water, cold
1 qt.	tomato sauce, your favorite
2 T	basil purée or pesto
½ cup	romano cheese
TT	kosher salt
TT	black pepper, coarse grind

Yield: 6 cups

Heat the olive oil in a 3-quart sauce pot over medium heat. Add the garlic, and sweat until translucent, DO NOT BROWN. Add the heavy cream, and bring it to a boil. Make a slurry by mixing the corn starch and cold water together until smooth. Whisk this into the cream. Once the cream is thick, add tomato sauce and basil purée. Bring to a simmer. Remove from the heat, and stir in romano cheese. Season with salt and pepper.

Warm Cider Dressing

This makes a spinach salad mouth watering and delicious! We like to use this with our spinach and arrugala salad. The sweetness of the reduced cider and the tanginess of the dijon blend to make a dressing that can also be used as a sauce for poultry, pork, and shrimp dishes alike.

2 T	butter, unsalted
1 ea	shallot, minced
1 ea	celery stalk, minced
1 T	garlic, minced
1 cup	heavy cream
1 tsp	ground cinnamon
2 T	dijon mustard
1 ½ cups	Cider Reduction*

Yield: 3 cups

In a small sauce pot, melt the butter over medium heat.

Add the shallots and celery, and sweat until translucent. Add the garlic, and stir for 30 seconds, DO NOT BROWN THE GARLIC!

Add the cinnamon and heavy cream, and reduce by ½. Add the dijon and the cider reduction, and bring them to a simmer. Remove from the heat, and let cool for about 10 minutes. Serve.

*Cider Reduction

½ gallon	apple cider
12 oz	V-8 juice

Yield: 1 ½ cups

Place both ingredients in a sauce pot over medium-high heat and reduce to 1 ½ cups.

Pineapple Chutney

This recipe works well with grilled fish or poultry. My favorite application is with grilled swordfish. Halibut, haddock, mahi mahi, and scallops are all good substitutes if you are not fond of swordfish.

Served over a grilled chicken breast or pork tenderloin are also good alternatives.

1 T	butter, unsalted
1/4 cup	red onion, small dice
1/4 cup	red peppers, small dice
1/2 tsp	fresh ginger, minced
1-16 oz can	pineapple chunks, drained well
3/4 cup	white wine vinegar
1/4 cup	white sugar
1/2 cup	brown sugar
1/2 tsp	kosher salt
1/2 cup	golden raisins

Yield: 3 cups

Melt the butter in a medium-sized saucepot. Add the onions, peppers, and ginger, and sauté over medium heat for 5 minutes, stirring frequently. Add the rest of the ingredients, and bring to a simmer.

Simmer for 45 minutes, stirring occasionally, and remove from the heat. Chill before serving. This will keep in the refrigerator for up to 3 weeks.

Demi Glace

A classical demi glace is ½ veal stock and ½ veal sauce reduced by half. This sauce is a reduction sauce and nothing more. We do not use a thickening agent of any kind. Here is how we do it at Keon's.

Take 1 qt of port wine and reduce it to 1 cup.

Follow the previous recipe for veal stock, combine it with the reduced port wine, and reduce to 1 ½ quarts.

Roasted Shallot Demi Glace

Take 1 cup of peeled shallots and lightly coat in oil. Sauté in a skillet until they are evenly browned. Place in a 375-degree oven for approximately 25 minutes. Remove from the oven, allow to cool and purée in a food processor. Add this mixture to 1 qt of Demi Glace. Season to taste.

Maple-Yogurt Dipping Sauce

This dipping sauce goes with the fried Butternut Squash Raviolis (page 110). It is also a good salad dressing for Spinach Salad with grilled chicken or steak. It makes a nice sauce when drizzled over grilled shrimp, salmon, or anything blackened.

¼ cup	Vermont maple syrup
½ cup	plain yogurt
½ cup	sour cream
¼ tsp	kosher salt
¼ tsp	black pepper, coarse grind
1 tsp	fresh chives, chopped

Yield: 1 ¼ cups

Mix all ingredients together and chill. Serve as needed.

Appetizers

Appetizers are fun to create. Typically, there are only a few components to complete the dish. For instance, our Texas Crab Cakes are a wonderful start to any meal. For the chef, you are prepping the crab cakes, aioli, and some salad greens. Therefore, at service time, there are only 2 components to worry about: searing the crab cakes and arranging the plate—because the Aioli is done ahead of time.

With entrées, there are many components to think about, and timing is more of an issue.

Appetizers are supposed to whet the appetite. Don't get into the habit of creating appetizers that are a substitute for the entrée. Even if the appetizer you are preparing is the best thing your guests have ever tasted, serve it in small amounts if a main course is to follow. You don't want your guests filling up on appetizers and leaving most of your entrée on the plate. It is always good to keep them wanting more. You women out there know what I mean!

Appetizers come in two categories: finger foods and plated appetizers. When hosting a dinner party, you might want to mix them. Serve a few finger foods first, and then have a plated appetizer to start the meal. In this case, remember not to serve too many of the passed appetizers. Keep your guests satisfied, but still wanting more.

Most of the recipes that follow are for plated appetizers. You can, however, take some of them, and turn them into passed appetizers. The crab cakes can be made ½ the size and served with a small dollop of aioli on top. The fritters are good finger food. The Tortilla Crusted Shrimp can be passed with the sauce as a dipping sauce. Be creative and have fun.

Baked Diver Scallops with Butternut Cream

This dish is one of our favorite appetizers. It looks great on the plate, and our guests always enjoy it. This scallop appetizer can also be served as an entrée. It goes well with an herbed risotto, wild rice, basmati rice (a long-grained white rice) and any variety of fresh vegetables. Thin out the butternut cream with Roasted Chicken Stock for a great soup starter.

When cooking with alcohol, always add it to the pan away from the stove and fire. When you return the pan to the stove, do so at arms length to avoid getting burned if the alcohol ignites.

Butternut Cream

1 T	butter, unsalted
2 ea	shallots, minced
½ cup	Sambuca
3–4 cups	butternut squash, peeled diced 1"
1 ½ cups	heavy cream
¼ tsp	kosher salt
¼ tsp	black pepper, coarse grind

Yield: 4–5 cups

In a 4-quart sauce pot, melt the butter over medium-high heat. Add the shallots, and sweat until translucent. Remove from the heat, and add the Sambuca. Return it to the stove, and reduce it until the liquid is almost all evaporated. Add the butternut squash and the cream along with the salt and pepper; simmer while covered, over medium heat, until the squash is tender. Purée in a food processor until smooth. Keep warm until needed.

Check seasoning.

Baked Scallops

2 T	canola oil
8 each	scallops, large dry
TT	kosher salt
TT	black pepper, coarse grind
½ cup	toasted fennel crumbs*
1 T	chopped chives

Yield: 4 portions

Heat a 10" skillet over high heat until the pan starts to smoke. Add the oil, and swirl it around carefully for about 30 seconds. Place the scallops in the pan, being careful there is some space between each one. Sauté until they are a deep golden brown. Turn over the scallops, and place the pan in a preheated 400-degree oven for approximately 4 minutes. Remove from oven, and turn on the broiler. Place the scallops in 6" baking dishes. Cover with 2 oz of the butternut squash mixture. Sprinkle the toasted fennel crumbs over the top, and put the dishes under the broiler until the crumbs are golden brown. Top with chopped chives and serve.

*Toasted Fennel Crumbs

1 T	butter, unsalted
pinch	ground fennel
1 cup	panko breadcrumbs

Yield: 8 portions

Melt the butter over medium heat, and add the fennel. When the butter starts to brown, add the breadcrumbs. Cook over low heat, stirring frequently, until the breadcrumbs are evenly browned.

Baked Littleneck Clams with Manchego and Crispy Shallots

Clams Casino is a classic dish that was popular for most of the latter half of the last century. Recently, chefs have become more daring with regards to spicing it up a bit with clams. This is one example. The clams are steamed, chilled, stuffed, and baked. The flavors combine to please the palate. The textures of the clam and the toasted breadcrumbs offer the guest a mouth-watering alternative to something fried or drowned in butter.

20 ea	littleneck clams or top neck clams, washed
½ cup	white wine
1 T	lemon juice
2 T	butter, unsalted
2 ea	shallots, minced
10 oz	crabmeat, fresh lump
½ tsp	Old Bay® Seasoning
TT	kosher salt
TT	black pepper, coarse grind
1 tsp	dijon mustard
2 T	white wine
1 T	lemon juice
¼ cup	panko breadcrumbs, toasted
20 ea	1" x 1" x ¼" thick slices of manchego cheese

Crispy Shallots

8 ea	sliced shallots, 1/8″ slices
As needed	all purpose flour
As needed	oil for frying
¾ cup	panko breadcrumbs

Yield: 4 portions

Steam the clams in the white wine and lemon juice until they open. Remove the clams from the shell. Split the shells, and discard half of them. Return the clams to the shells you have saved and set aside.

For Crispy Shallots

Take the sliced shallots, and be sure that the rings are all separated. Dust them in flour, and fry in hot oil until crispy. Strain and season with salt and pepper.

For the Filling

Melt the butter In a medium-sized skillet. Add the shallots, and sweat until translucent. Add the crabmeat, Old Bay®, dijon mustard, white wine, lemon juice and season to taste. Heat until warmed through. Mix well, and remove from the heat. Mix in the breadcrumbs.

Put a lump of the crabmeat filling on each of the clams. Cover with a slice of the manchego, and bake at 350 degrees for 2 minutes or until the cheese has melted. Sprinkle the breadcrumbs over all of the clams, and put them under the broiler to brown. Serve on a plate with the crispy shallots in the center.

Duck Confit

Duck confit is made with duck legs. It is a delicacy that can be found all over France. The process for duck confit has remained the same for hundreds of years. The purpose is to help preserve the duck and its flavors through curing. Once the duck has been cured for 36-48 hours. It is then poached in its own fat until tender and flavorful. Duck confit can be stored in the refrigerator for up to 6 months. I like to eat it when it comes out of the oven. I mean, why wait?

The fat from the confit is an excellent medium for pan-fried potatoes. The flavor it adds is incredible.

3 T	kosher salt
1 T	fresh chopped garlic
1 T	black pepper, coarse grind
1 tsp	dry thyme leaves
8 ea	duck legs
1 cup	duck fat

Yield: 8 portions

Mix together the salt, garlic, pepper, and thyme. Rub evenly over the 8 duck legs, and keep this in the refrigerator for 36-48 hours.

Wipe off the salt mixture, and sear the duck legs with the skin side down in a shallow, wide pot. Once the duck legs are seared and golden brown, remove from the heat, and add the cup of duck fat. Place in a 250-degree oven until the meat falls off the bone. The cooking time can vary from 3-5 hours.

Once the meat is tender, remove the pot from the oven, and serve or allow the confit to cool in the fat. Storage of confit is always done in the fat to help preserve its shelf life and flavors. Once the confit is cool, transfer to a storage container, and be sure the duck is completely submerged in the fat.

Grilled Corn and Potato Fritters

½ cup	Grilled Corn (page 184)
1 cup	Whipped Yukon Potatoes, cold (page 194)
2 ea	eggs
1 cup	milk, cold
¼ tsp	cayenne pepper
½ tsp	kosher salt
¼ tsp	black pepper, table grind
1/3 cup	flour
2 tsp	baking powder

Yield: Approximately 25 fritters

In a medium bowl, mix the cold mashed potatoes, eggs, milk, cayenne, salt, and pepper until smooth. Sift the baking powder and flour together, and add it to the potato mixture. Fold in the Grilled Corn. Let stand 15 minutes.

Drop teaspoon-sized dollops of the mixture into a 350-degree fryer, and cook them until the edges are golden brown, about 2 minutes. Using a fork, turn the fritters over so the uncooked side is now facing down, and continue to cook for about 1 minute. Remove, and place them on paper towels to absorb the excess grease. Season with salt and pepper.

These are wonderful when drizzled with honey!

Grilled Fontina Marinated Shrimp

This dish makes a good appetizer, salad, entrée, or finger food. The flavors are bold and delicious.

For an entrée, they go well with rice pilaf or any good rice dish, risotto, whipped Yukon Potatoes, etc. Personally, I prefer these shrimp on a salad lightly dressed with my Citrus Vinaigrette.

2 T	lemon juice, fresh
2 T	lime juice, fresh
1/3 cup	orange juice, fresh
1 tsp	dijon mustard
1 tsp	honey
¼ cup	red onions, fine dice
2 tsp	fresh dill, chopped
½ cup	fontina cheese, ¼" dice
½ tsp	kosher salt
¾ tsp	black pepper, coarse grind
1 cup	extra virgin olive oil
1 lb	U–16 shrimp, peeled and veins removed
¼ cup	olive oil
1 T	fresh garlic, chopped
16 ea	french bread slices, ½" thick

Yield: 16 crostinis

In a medium-sized bowl, whisk the first 10 ingredients together. Then, slowly drizzle in the first olive oil in a slow stream while whisking.

Check seasoning.

Pour this mixture over the shrimp, and allow it to marinate for 24 hours.

Heat the second olive oil in a small sauté pan, and add the garlic. Cook until translucent, about 1 minute.

Remove the garlic oil from the heat. Brush it lightly onto the 16 pieces of french bread.

Place the bread slices on a cookie sheet. Bake at 375 degrees for 6-8 minutes, or until golden brown around the edges. Remove from the oven, and turn the broiler on.

Remove the shrimp from the marinade, and wipe off any excess oil before grilling, as it will cause your shrimp to get a black residue from all the extra oil hitting the coals.

Grill the shrimp for 2 minutes on one side, and turn them over for 1 minute. Remove them from the grill, and place them on a cookie sheet close together. Spoon the cheese and vegetable mixture over the shrimp, and place them under the broiler to melt the cheese. This will take approximately 3-4 minutes. Taste one for seasoning. Hey, you're the cook, tasting is one of the benefits!

Season if necessary. Slice each of the shrimp lengthwise, and place both halves of a shrimp atop each of the Crostinis. Bake at 375 degrees for a minute or two, if necessary.

Grilled Polenta with Roasted Peppers and Fresh Mozzarella

I like this dish because most of the prep can be done well in advance. You can have the polenta already cooked, cooled, and ready to grill. The roasted peppers can be done the day before, and the fresh mozzarella can be sliced ahead of time. So when you have guests coming over, and you want to start them with a great tasting appetizer, this is the recipe.

Polenta should be made a day ahead.

1 T	olive oil
³/₄ cup	red onion, small dice
1 tsp	fresh garlic, chopped
1 cup	Grilled Corn (page 184)
3 cups	milk
1 tsp	kosher salt
1 cup	cornmeal, stone ground
¹/₄ cup	parmesan cheese, grated
¹/₄ cup	romano cheese, grated

Yield: 8 portions

Heat the olive oil in a skillet. Add the red onion, and sauté for 5 minutes, or until they becomes translucent. Add the chopped garlic, and sauté an additional minute. Add the Grilled Corn, and continue cooking for additional 3 minutes, or until the mixture is hot.

Bring 2 cups of milk and the salt to a boil over a medium heat. Mix the remaining cold milk with the cornmeal until smooth. Then, add it to the boiling milk. Cook over low heat until smooth, stirring frequently with a wooden spoon. This will take approximately 30 minutes. Stir in the warm Grilled Corn mixture. Stir in both cheeses. Remove from heat.

Brush an 8"x 8" pan with olive oil, and pour the warm polenta mix into it. Spread evenly with a spatula or wooden spoon. Let cool at room temperature for 30 minutes, and then cool in the refrigerator.

8 oz	roasted red and yellow peppers
8–1 oz	fresh mozzarella slices
2 T	extra virgin olive oil
3 T	basil chiffonade

Cut the chilled polenta into 4 even squares and then again diagonally into even triangles. Brush lightly with olive oil. Place on a very hot, clean, and oiled grill to get good grill marks. Remove from the grill, and place on a greased cookie sheet. Divide the roasted peppers evenly over all of the polenta pieces. Place a slice of fresh mozzarella atop each of the polenta triangles. Brush with extra virgin olive oil. Place in a 375-degree oven for 5-7 minutes to heat, allowing the mozzarella to melt.

Garnish with basil chiffonade.

Keon's Bread Spread

Our bread spread came to be as a way to differentiate us from the competition.

Twenty years ago or so extra virgin olive oil was served at the tables of many fine dining restaurants. It was served with style and panache. The oil would be blended with fresh herbs and seasonings and maybe some grated parmesan or romano cheese. When served correctly, with warm bread, it was incredible. Unfortunately, as time went by most restaurants went to cheaper oils and dried herbs.

I decided to go in another direction all together. I wanted to make bread dips. They would change weekly, and I could get as creative as I wanted. I did this for a year or so.

But, when I started serving the lemon- basil hummus, it was such a hit that we have not changed it. Below is the recipe for our lemon-basil hummus (Keon's Bread Spread) and a few others. They are all worth trying.

1 ea	16 oz can chic peas
1 oz	lemon juice
3/4 tsp	fresh garlic, chopped
1/2 tsp	kosher salt
1/4 tsp	black pepper, coarse grind
1 T	basil chiffonade, firmly packed
3 oz	80/20 oil blend

Yield: 2 1/2 cups

Place all ingredients in a food processor, and purée until smooth. Shut off the processor every once in a while, and scrape the sides to be sure there aren't any lumps.

Red Pepper Bread Dip

Follow the Keon's Bread Spread but only use 2 oz of the oil blend, and add ¼ cup of roasted red peppers. Blend until smooth.

Roasted Eggplant Bread Dip

Follow the Keon's Bread Spread, but only use 2 oz of the oil blend. Add ½ cup of roasted eggplant.

Roasted Eggplant

To roast the eggplant, poke it in a few places with a fork and place in a 400-degree oven for 30 minutes. Once the eggplant is cooked, remove it from the oven, remove the flash from the skin using a spoon, and discard the flesh. Put the eggplant flesh in the food processor until smooth.

Spinach and Oven Roasted Tomato Bread Dip

6 ea	Oven Roasted Tomatoes (page 186)
½ cup	baby spinach, blanched

Following the Keon's Bread Spread, place all of the ingredients (except the chic peas) in a food processor along with the blanched spinach and the Oven Roasted Tomatoes.

Purée until smooth. Add the chic peas, and purée them until smooth. Check seasoning and serve.

Lobster and Chanterelle Stuffed Artichoke Hearts

This appetizer is easy to prep and serve. Your guests will love this, and so will you.

2 T	butter, unsalted
2 T	shallots, minced
6 oz	fresh chanterelle mushrooms, cut small
2 T	roasted red peppers, diced small
10 oz	lobster meat, fresh, par cooked, cut into 3/4" pieces
TT	kosher salt
TT	black pepper, coarse grind
8 ea	artichoke hearts, canned
4 oz	Hollandaise Sauce (page 53)
1 tsp	fresh chopped chives

Yield: 4 portions

Melt the butter in a small sauté pan over medium-high heat. Add the shallots and the chanterelles, and sauté for 2-3 minutes. Add the roasted peppers, and toss together. Add the lobster meat and seasoning, and continue to cook until the lobster is hot throughout. This will only take 2 minutes or so. Do not overcook the lobster, as it will become tough. Remove from the heat, and allow to cool.

Open the artichokes delicately, and fill with the lobster/chanterelle stuffing. You should have stuffing left over to use for garnishing the plate.

When you are ready to serve, have the Hollandaise warm and ready. Place the artichokes on a greased cookie sheet, and bake in a 375-degree oven. Bake for 3 minutes. Put the extra filling on the sheet, and bake it for an additional 3-4 minutes. Arrange 2 stuffed artichokes on a plate, and napé with Hollandaise sauce. Garnish with some chopped chives. Arrange some of the extra filling around the artichokes for appearance.

Roasted Tomato and Goat Cheese Tart

This is good any time of year. I prefer to use vine-ripened tomatoes as they tend to have a much richer flavor than hot house tomatoes. The key to this one coming out as planned is to take your time roasting the tomatoes, which can and should be done in advance.

4 ea	puff pastry squares, uncooked, 5" x 5"
As needed	egg wash
8 ea	Oven Roasted Tomato Halves (page 186)
2 T	roasted yellow peppers, julienne
3 T	goat cheese
4 tsp	extra virgin olive oil
1/4 tsp	black pepper, coarse grind
1/4 tsp	kosher salt
1 tsp	basil chiffonade

Yield: 4 portions

First, lay out the puff pastry squares on a parchment-lined cookie sheet. Brush a little egg wash around the edges of all of the puff squares. Now fold over 1/2" of the puff pastry so that you have an edge around the entire square. The dough will now be roughly 4" squares with a double layer border around the edge of each. Brush the border with a thin layer of egg wash, and bake at 400 degrees for 15 minutes. Remove from the oven, and push the centers down flat so that the borders are now raised above the center.

Next, arrange 2 tomato halves in the center of each puff pastry. Evenly distribute the roasted peppers, goat cheese, olive oil, salt, and pepper over the 4 squares. Return them to the oven for 5 minutes. Remove from the oven. The puff pastry should be golden brown, and the filling nice and hot. Garnish with the chiffonade of basil and serve.

Romano Chicken Fingers
with Sun Dried Tomato Risotto

This is one of the more popular appetizers we have served at Keon's. It combines textures, flavors and color. Whenever you can accomplish that, the dish has a greater chance of success. It is a challenge during busy service, because there are three steps and three pans to prepare the dish. At home, this dish should not pose any problems.

I recommend that you have the sauce and risotto done and held warm when the chicken fingers go in the pan.

8 ea	chicken fingers, tendons removed
TT	kosher salt
TT	black pepper, coarse grind
As needed	flour for breading
2 ea	eggs
2 oz	cold water
½ cup	romano cheese
1 cup	panko breadcrumbs
½ cup	80/20 blend oil
8 oz	Pink Pomodoro Sauce (page 59)
12 oz	Sun Dried Tomato Risotto (page 192)
1 T	basil chiffonade
1 T	romano cheese, grated

Yield: 4 portions

Combine the eggs and water in a medium-sized bowl to make an egg wash. Combine the romano cheese and the breadcrumbs in a medium-sized bowl for the breading.

Season the chicken fingers with salt and pepper. Dredge in flour, dip into the egg wash, and bread in the breading mixture.

Heat the oil in a large, non stick skillet, and brown the chicken fingers on both sides. Finish in a 350-degree oven if necessary.

Place 3 oz of risotto in the center of each of 4 plates. Pour 2 oz of the Pink Pomodoro Sauce around the risotto. Crisscross the chicken fingers over the risotto. Garnish with basil chiffonade and grated romano.

Steamed Mussels in Curried-Carrot Broth

Steamed mussels are a wonderful way to start a dinner. They offer a way to excite the palate. This recipe will wake the taste buds with flavors that are both sweet and savory.

Be sure to serve a nice loaf of warm bread with this dish as your guests will be sopping up all the juices when finished.

For the Curried-Carrot Broth

1 T	butter, unsalted
1 cup	carrots, chopped small
1/4 cup	yellow onions, chopped small
2 ea	cloves of garlic
2 tsp	fresh ginger, chopped
2 oz	white wine
6 oz	Roasted Chicken Stock (page 143)
1 ea	thyme sprig
1/4 tsp	kosher salt
1/8 tsp	black pepper, coarse grind
1 oz	heavy cream
3 oz	butter, unsalted

For the Mussels

1 T	canola oil
4 lbs	mussels, I prefer Prince Edward Island mussels
2 T	parsley, chopped

Yield: 4 portions

In a small sauce pot, melt the butter over medium-high heat. Add the carrots, onions, garlic, and ginger, and sweat the vegetables for about 5 minutes. Add the rest of the ingredients, and bring them to a simmer. Allow this to simmer for 30 minutes. Remove the sprig of thyme, and purée in a food processor. When smooth, put the mixture back in a saucepot over medium heat, and whisk in the heavy cream and butter. Once the butter has been absorbed, remove from the heat and keep warm until ready for use.

For Service

Heat the oil in a large skillet over a high flame. When the oil is hot, add ¼ of the mussels with a splash of white wine and cover. Cook until the mussels open, approximately 3 minutes. Remove the lid, and add ¼ of the carrot mixture. Toss well and serve. I like to garnish these with some chopped parsley.

Texas Crab Cakes

Crab cakes are a staple at many restaurants up and down the east coast of the United States. That being said, I cannot emphasize enough the importance of serving only the best. Use only fresh lump crabmeat.

Some restaurants serve their crab cakes fried, some serve theirs pan seared or sautéed. I like to pan sear ours in a very hot pan in a thin layer of oil. I find they are never greasy and always maintain that high level of quality.

1 lb	crab meat, fresh lump
2 T	red peppers, small dice
2 T	green peppers, small dice
1 ea	jalapeños
2 T	cilantro, chopped
2 T	lime juice
¼ cup	extra heavy mayo
½ cup	panko breadcrumbs
1 T	Old Bay® Seasoning
¼ tsp	cayenne pepper (optional)
TT	kosher salt
TT	black pepper, coarse grind
As needed	all purpose flour
½ cup	oil for sautéing

Yield: 16–1 ½ oz crab cakes

In a large mixing bowl, combine all ingredients. Form into approximately 1 ½ oz cakes. Lightly coat the cakes in flour.

Heat the oil in a sauté pan, and brown the crab cakes on both sides to a golden brown. Place the crab cakes in a 350–degree oven for approximately 3 minutes. Serve with Pico di Gallo Mayonnaise (page 57).

Tortilla Crusted Shrimp
with Sweet Corn-Serrano Sauce

This dish has a bit of a southwest flair. I thoroughly enjoyed working in Dallas' Crescent Court Hotel. The dishes prepared there were always bursting with bold flavors. This is no different. I'm not sure exactly who came up with the original idea for this, but here is my version.

1 ½ cups	white tortilla chips, ground fine in a food processor (low salt)
½ cup	panko breadcrumbs
¼ tsp	ground cumin
¼ tsp	ground turmeric
¼ tsp	cayenne pepper
¼ tsp	black pepper, coarse grind
12 ea	U-12 shrimp, peeled and deveined
TT	kosher salt
TT	black pepper, coarse grind
As needed	flour, for breading
2 ea	eggs
3 T	cold water
As needed	oil for frying, 350 degrees
8 oz	Sweet Corn-Serrano Sauce (page 58)
8 oz	Grilled Corn and Black Bean Salsa (page 185)
1 T	cilantro, chopped
4 ea	large lime wedges

Yield: 4 portions

continues next page...

Mix the ground tortilla chips, breadcrumbs, cumin, turmeric, cayenne pepper, and black pepper together in a large bowl.

Season the shrimp. Dust the shrimp lightly in flour. Dip them into the egg wash, then into the tortilla mixture. Fry at 350 degrees for approximately 3 minutes, or until done. Do not over cook.

Sometimes it is best to fry for 1 ½-2 minutes and finish them in a 350-degree oven to avoid over browning.

Take 2 oz of the Grilled Corn Salsa, and make a mound in the center of the serving plate. Take 2 oz of the Sweet Corn-Serrano Sauce. Pour this around the salsa to fill the plate between the salsa and the rim. Place the shrimp at 12, 4 and 8 o'clock on the plate with the tails crossing at the center.

Garnish with chopped cilantro and a lime wedge.

Soups and Salads

The key to a good soup is to start with a good, rich stock. If your stock or broth lacks sufficient flavor, then so will your soup. I like to make my own stocks for soup. The recipes for my stocks are on the following pages and are easy to produce. Planning ahead is important, as a good stock will take hours of stove time even though the prep time is short.

If you don't have the time to make your own stock, or you prefer to use a base or broth, then be sure to use one that is of the highest quality. Powdered bases tend to be salty in flavor and have a chemical taste to them. Avoid them at all costs. There are a few bases that come in paste form. They tend to be better than powder bases. I'm still not a fan of them, but if you must, you must.

Seasoning is the next step to produce a soup with flavors that will make your guests say, "Wow!" Salt and pepper should always be used to enhance your finished product. Fresh herbs will make a soup taste better. When using fresh herbs, understand that their flavor tends to diminish over time. When you reheat a soup the following day or a few days later, additional fresh herbs may be needed to give the freshness you are looking for—usually half as much as the original recipe called for.

The colors in a soup are also important. When your guest sees a soup that has good color, it will increase their anticipation and almost always make the product taste better. You will hear me talk of color throughout the book. If food looks good, it will taste good.

The base of almost all soups is celery, carrots, and onions. This gives a good, rich flavor to begin with. Sometimes, as with New England clam chowder or fish chowder, carrots will be omitted. Whenever possible, keep the carrots in there for both color and flavor. One mistake that is often made when making soup is the celery, carrots, and onions are not sweated before adding the stock. Sweating the vegetables brings out their sweetness, especially with onions. Sweating onions turns the sulfides into sugar, making a much better flavor for soups.

Producing a good soup is easy once you have a feel for it. Do not get in the habit of making a soup pot your "catch-all" for everything in the refrigerator. Follow the same recipes or guidelines to produce consistent soups. That is not to say you can't add or change any recipe that you wish. But, if you are trying to produce soups for regular clientele, as opposed to a few guests once in a while, then consistency is imperative for success.

Classically, in Europe, salads were served after the main course. The thought behind it was the salad greens aided in digestion. I've never found out if this is actually true. I love salads, before, after, or during the main course. I am not a fan of salads that do not have substance. By this I mean, nuts, olives, poached pears, orange segments, anything that will give the salad a twist. That is why I serve my Caesar salad with marinated tomatoes. I love a good Caesar, but give me something more than lettuce. Again, be creative when making your salads. Add something to it.

Melt the butter in an 8-quart saucepot over medium heat. Add the shallots, and sweat until translucent. Add the brown sugar, and stir until melted. Add the butternut squash, Roasted Chicken Stock, rosemary, marjoram, cinnamon, salt, and pepper. Bring to a boil, and reduce to a simmer. Simmer for 30 minutes. Remove from the heat and purée the soup in a blender in small batches until smooth. Be careful when puréeing hot liquids in a blender, as the pressure can blow the cap off. To avoid this, fill the blender half-way or less, and drape a cloth over the top to avoid being scalded. Hold the cap on tight while puréeing.

Combine the heavy cream and the eggs yolks in a medium-sized bowl. Take a ladle of the puréed soup, and whisk it into the cream mixture. Now, whisk the cream mixture into the pot of soup. Return the soup to the stove over a medium heat for 1 minute, stirring constantly. The soup will thicken slightly. Remove from the heat, check seasoning, and serve.

Cream of Asparagus and Roasted Red Pepper Soup

This is a great winter soup. It is easy to make and quick to prepare. Remember to have a loaf of warm bread nearby to fully enjoy this soup. It is also important to peel the broccoli stems before chopping them.

1 T	butter, unsalted
½ cup	yellow onion, small dice
¼ cup	celery, small dice
1 qt	Roasted Chicken Stock (page 143)
2 cups	fresh medium asparagus, chopped small
1 cup	roasted red peppers, store-bought, drained well, puréed
3 T	butter, unsalted, softened
3 T	flour
1 ½ cups	heavy cream
TT	kosher salt
TT	black pepper, coarse grind

Yield: 8–10 portions

Melt the first butter in a 12-quart sauce pot. Add the onion and celery, and sweat until translucent. Add the Roasted Chicken Stock, chopped asparagus, and the puréed roasted red peppers. Bring to a boil, and reduce to a simmer for 25 minutes.

Blend the flour and the second butter together until smooth. Add this to the soup while whisking vigorously. It will take a minute or so for this to melt into the soup. Once the lumps have disappeared, let the soup simmer over a low heat for 5 minutes. Remove from the heat, and purée in a blender in small batches. Return the puréed soup to the heat, and add the cream. Bring the soup back to a simmer, and check seasonings.

Corn and Artichoke Chowder

As with New England clam chowder, the trick to this chowder is to keep a constant eye on it during the cooking process. Once you have added and cooked the flour, the soup will want to stick to the bottom of your pot. If it becomes necessary, change pots during the cooking process to prevent any char flavor tainting your chowder.

3 slices	apple wood bacon, 1/8" julienne (breakfast bacon can substitute)
¼ cup	butter, unsalted
1 ea	large yellow onion, ¼" dice
3 ea	celery ribs, ¼" dice
½ cup	carrots, ¼" dice
¼ cup	all purpose flour
1 ½ qts	Roasted Chicken Stock (page 143)
½ cup	roasted red peppers, puréed
3 cups	Idaho potatoes, ½" dice
1 ½ cups	fresh or frozen corn
1–16oz can	artichoke hearts, chopped ½"
1 ½ cups	heavy cream
2 tsp	kosher salt
1 tsp	black pepper, coarse grind
1 T	parsley, fresh, chopped

Yield: 1 gallon

In an 8-quart sauce pot, cook the julienne bacon slices until crispy, stirring frequently. Add the butter and the diced onion, and sweat over medium–high heat until translucent. This will take about 5 minutes. Add the celery and carrots, and sweat for an additional 4 minutes. Add the flour and stir with a wooden spoon until it has all been incorporated evenly into the fat and vegetables. Reduce heat to medium, and cook for 3-4 minutes stirring constantly. Add the Roasted Chicken Stock and roasted red peppers, and whisk until the stock is smooth and without lumps, scraping the bottom of the pot to prevent sticking. Bring the soup to a simmer, and add the diced potatoes. Reduce the heat to low, and simmer for 20 minutes, stirring occasionally. The potatoes will settle to the bottom and stick if you are not careful. Add the corn and the chopped artichoke hearts, and simmerfor 10 minutes. Add the cream, salt, and pepper, and continue to simmer for 5 more minutes. Add the chopped parsley, and check the seasoning before serving. Add salt and pepper if necessary.

Fish Chowder

As with New England clam chowder, the trick to this chowder is to keep a constant eye on it during the cooking process. Once you have added and cooked the flour, the soup will want to stick to the bottom of your pot. If it becomes necessary, change pots during the cooking process to prevent any char flavor tainting your chowder.

3 slices	apple wood bacon, 1/8" julienne (breakfast bacon can substitute)
¼ cup	butter, unsalted
1 ea	large yellow onion, ¼" dice
3 ea	celery ribs, ¼" dice
½ tsp	dry parsley leaves
¼ cup	all purpose flour
5 cups	Fish Stock (page 142)
3 cups	Idaho potatoes, ½" dice
1 lb	cod, haddock, or pollack, cut into 2" pieces
1 ½ cups	heavy cream
2 tsp	kosher salt
1 tsp	black pepper, coarse grind
1 T	chopped fresh parsley

Yield: 1 gallon

In an 8-quart sauce pot, cook the julienne bacon slices until crispy, stirring frequently. Add the butter, diced onion, celery, and dried parsley, and sweat over medium-high heat until translucent. This will take about 5 minutes. Add the flour, and stir with a wooden spoon until it has all been incorporated evenly into the fat and vegetables. Reduce heat to medium, and cook for 3-4 minutes, stirring constantly. Add the Fish Stock, and whisk until the stock is smooth and without lumps, scraping the bottom of the pot to prevent sticking. Bring the soup to a simmer and add the diced potatoes. Reduce the heat to low, and simmer for 20 minutes, stirring occasionally. The potatoes will settle to the bottom and stick if you are not careful. Add the fish, and simmer 20 more minutes, stirring occasionally. Add the cream, salt, and pepper, and continue to simmer for 5 more minutes. Add the chopped parsley, and check the seasoning before serving. Add salt and pepper if necessary.

French Onion Soup

As I mentioned at the beginning of this chapter, the key to a good soup is good stock.

I like to use both Chicken and Veal stock for my onion soup. If you don't have the time to make your own stocks, then get a good, high-quality base, and follow the instructions on the package. If you do use a base, taste the stock before you add it to the soup. Be sure there is sufficient flavor. If it tastes too watery, add a little more of the base to enhance its flavor.

For a really good onion soup, the onions must be caramelized properly. This takes an hour or more. Proper caramelizing of the onions will give your soup a deep rich color and flavor. Do not rush the caramelizing process.

4 oz	butter, unsalted
5 lbs	yellow onions, peeled, core removed, and cut into ¼" slices
1 cup	red wine
½ cup	sherry
2 ½ pints	Roasted Chicken Stock (page 143)
2 ½ pints	Veal Stock (page 144)
6 sprigs	fresh thyme
2 ea	bay leaves
1 T	kosher salt
2 tsp	black pepper, coarse grind

Yield: 8 portions

In a large stockpot, melt the butter, and add the onions. Sweat for 15 minutes over medium-low heat without stirring. The onions should be evenly browned on the bottom of the pot. Now, stir them just enough to get the bottom onions to the top and others to the bottom for caramelizing. Over-stirring will result in juices from the onions seeping into the pot and slowing the caramelizing process. Continue this process until the onions are evenly caramelized. Do not cheat! Be sure all of the onions have good, rich color before adding any liquid.

Once the onions are sufficiently caramelized, add the sherry and the red wine, and increase the heat to high. Stir occasionally until most of the liquid has evaporated.

Add the rest of the ingredients, and bring to a boil. Reduce heat to medium, and allow to simmer for 30 minutes. Check the seasoning and serve with a swiss cheese crouton on top.

For the Croutons

| 8 ea | slices of french bread, cut diagonally ½″ thick |
| 8 ea | thin slices of swiss or gruyere cheese |

While the soup is simmering, place the 8 pieces of bread in a 400-degree oven, and allow to crisp and the edges to brown. This will take 6-8 minutes. Place a slice of the swiss cheese on each of the browned croutons, and place under the broiler until golden brown. Be careful not to have any exposed edges of bread as it will burn before the cheese browns.

Lemon-Pepper Chicken Soup

This is, and has always been, a favorite of mine! I like it because there are so many variations you can make with it.

2 T	butter, unsalted
1 cup	yellow onions, 1/4" dice
1/2 cup	celery, 1/4" dice
1/2 cup	carrots, 1/4" dice
3/4 cup	lemon grass, rinsed and dried, 1/2" chopped
1/3 cup	orzo
1 T	lemon juice
1 1/2 qts	Roasted Chicken Stock (page 143)
1 1/2 cups	cooked chicken, 1/2" dice
1 T	black pepper, coarse grind
1 T	fresh parsley, chopped, is best (dry will do)
1/2 cup	heavy cream

Yield: 8 portions

Melt the butter in an 8-quart stock pot. Add the onions, and sweat until translucent. Add the celery, carrots, and lemon grass. Cook over medium-high heat for 5 minutes, stirring occasionally.

Add the lemon juice and Roasted Chicken Stock, and bring to a boil. Add the orzo, and boil for 20 minutes. Reduce to a simmer, and add the chicken, pepper, and parsley. Simmer an additional 10 minutes, and stir in the cream. Season if necessary.

Buffalo Chicken Soup

This is an easy one that tastes great! Follow the above recipe; add ¼ cup of light brown sugar and 3 T of Frank's Red Hot Sauce° with the Roasted Chicken Stock. You can increase the hot sauce to your liking.

New England Clam Chowder

The trick to this chowder is to keep a constant eye on it during the cooking process. Once you have added and cooked the flour, the soup will want to stick to the bottom of your pot. If it becomes necessary, change pots during the cooking process to prevent any char flavor tainting your chowder.

3 slices	apple wood bacon, 1/8" julienne (breakfast bacon can substitute)
1/4 cup	butter, unsalted
1 ea	large yellow onion, 1/4" dice
3 ea	celery ribs, 1/4" dice
1/2 tsp	dry thyme leaves
1/4 cup	all purpose flour
1 ea	46 oz can of diced clams in juice, or equal amount of smaller cans
5 cups	Idaho potatoes, 1/2" dice
1 1/2 cups	heavy cream
2 tsp	kosher salt
1 tsp	black pepper, coarse grind
1 T	parsley, fresh, chopped

Yield: 1 gallon

In an 8-quart sauce pot, cook the julienne bacon slices until crispy, stirring frequently. Add the butter, diced onion, celery, and thyme leaves, and sweat for an additional 5-6 minutes. Add the flour, and stir with a wooden spoon until it has all been incorporated evenly throughout the vegetables. Reduce heat to medium, and cook for 3-4 minutes, stirring constantly. Add the diced clams and juice, and whisk until the stock is smooth and without lumps. Bring the chowder to a simmer and add the diced potatoes. Simmer over low heat for 20 minutes, stirring frequently. The potatoes will settle and stick to the bottom if left unattended. Add the cream, salt, and pepper, and continue to simmer for 5 more minutes. Add the chopped parsley, and check seasoning before serving.

Bibb Salad

This is a nice, light salad. It is the perfect start to a meal. Bibb lettuce, also known as Boston lettuce, is very mellow in flavor. Its leaves are soft and pleasing to the palate.

I like to use a hydro bib lettuce. This is a lettuce that has been grown in water. The leaves and heads are consistent in size and flavor. Also, there is no dirt in the roots to worry about.

Be careful not to overdress a salad using bib lettuce, as it will absorb the dressing quickly and become soggy. Adding roasted red and/or yellow peppers will give this plate more color and flavor.

2 each	hydro bibb lettuce, root removed
4 oz	Honey-Champagne Vinaigrette (page 55)
TT	kosher salt
TT	black pepper, coarse grind
28 ea	Spiced Pecans (page 191)
4 ea	¼" thick wedge of Great Hill Blue cheese
1 ea	poached pear, quartered, sliced
4 ea	red onion, very thin slices

Yield: 4 portions

Separate the bib leaves, and put them in a large mixing bowl with 4 oz of Honey-Champagne Vinaigrette. Season lightly with salt and pepper, and mix the lettuce leaves and dressing until they are evenly coated. Remove the leaves from the bowl, and arrange them on 4 separate plates, piling them high.

Place 7 Spiced Pecans and 1 slice of the red pepper on each salad, and spread the pear slices evenly over each of the salads as well. Next, lay a wedge of the Great Hill Blue cheese against the side of each salad and serve.

Keon's Caesar Salad

A classic Caesar salad is romaine, Caesar Dressing, croutons, and anchovies.

I find that the majority of our customers are not fond of anchovies sitting on top of their salad. For that reason, we only use them in the dressing.

I find a Caesar to be boring. I want some substance and color in my salad. For this reason, I add Marinated Cherry Tomatoes. You can also add roasted red peppers, shaved red onions, kalamata olives, etc. Try to think outside the box, and your guests will always be pleased.

3 ea	hearts of romaine, cut into 1 1/2" pieces
4 oz	Keon's Caesar Dressing (page 32)
4 oz	croutons, freshly baked
6 oz	Marinated Cherry Tomatoes (page 186)
1 oz	parmesan cheese, shredded
1/4 tsp	black pepper, coarse grind

Yield: 4 salads

Mix the romaine, croutons, and the dressing in a large bowl. Divide evenly over 4 plates, and pile high. Place the Marinated Cherry Tomatoes randomly atop the salad, and sprinkle with the shredded parmesan cheese. Sprinkle the coarse ground black pepper over the salad and serve.

Frisée Salad with Duck Confit and Blood Orange Vinaigrette

When you really want to impress, this one's a winner. Duck confit is comfort food. When combined with frisée lettuce and the Blood Orange Vinaigrette, you have a winner. As I talked about in the beginning of the book, color and texture are so important in cooking. Here, you have bright colors with varying textures. And the flavors are incredible! I'm not a fan of making my guests work too hard to eat. For that reason, I suggest that you cut the frisée into bite-sized pieces.

4 ea	heads of baby frisée lettuce, or 2 large heads, stems removed, leaves separated
5 oz	Blood Orange Vinaigrette (page 30)
1/4 tsp	kosher salt
1/4 tsp	black pepper, coarse grind
2 T	red onions, shaved
6 ea	Oven Roasted Tomato halves, julienne
2 T	carrots, shaved
2 T	julienne radish
1/4 cup	Spiced Pecans, chopped (page 191)
12 oz	Duck Confit (page 68)

Yield: 4 portions

If you have made the confit in advance, place the 12 ozs on a cookie sheet in a 350-degree oven for 4-5 minutes to warm.

In a large bowl, mix the frisée with the Blood Orange Vinaigrette. Season with the salt and pepper, and toss well so that the dressing is evenly distributed. Arrange the dressed frisée onto 4 plates. Sprinkle the shaved onions, tomato julienne, shaved carrots, radish julienne, and Spiced Pecans over the tops of each salad.

Take 3 ozs of warmed Duck Confit, and place this in a mound in the center of each salad. Serve.

Iceberg Wedge with Great Hill Blue Cheese and Apple Smoked Bacon

Typically, I am not a fan of iceberg lettuce. But, as with all ingredients, there is a time and a place to use them, and no substitution will do. This is a hearty salad with bold flavors that compliment the mundane flavor of iceberg lettuce.

1 ea	medium-sized head of iceberg lettuce
4 ea	wedges of Great Hill Blue cheese
8 oz	Aioli (page 26)
1 T	lemon juice
1 T	basil purée
8 ea	apple smoked bacon slices, cooked, julienne
½ cup	roasted red peppers, julienne
¼ cup	red onion, shaved
16 each	Marinated Cherry Tomatoes, halved (page 186)

Yield: 4 portions

Quarter the iceberg lettuce, wash, and shake off any excess water. Wrap in paper towels for about 15 minutes. Place the lettuce in the center of the plate, and lean the wedge of Great Hill Blue cheese against the lettuce.

In a small bowl, mix the lemon juice, Aioli, and basil purée. Pesto can be substituted for the basil purée.

Napé 2 oz of the Aioli mixture over the iceberg wedge, and garnish the salad with ¼ of the bacon, roasted peppers, onions, and tomatoes.

Grilled Corn can be added for extra flavor and color.

Spinach and Arrugala Salad
with Warm Cider Dressing

This salad is a great winter salad, although, I enjoy it year-round. The cider dressing should be warm, not boiling. The idea is to slightly wilt the greens. If you have a thermometer nearby, the dressing should be at 140 degrees. This way, once it hits the cold greens, is plated and served, your guests will enjoy something that is just warmer than room temperature.

4 oz	baby spinach
4 oz	baby arrugala
2 oz	Warm Cider Dressing (page 60)
TT	kosher salt
TT	black pepper, coarse grind
1 oz	red onions, shaved
6 pcs	apple smoked bacon, cooked and julienne
12 ea	Marinated Cherry Tomatoes, halved (page 186)
2 T	carrots, shaved
20 ea	Smoked Gouda Croutons (page 188)

Yield: 4 salads

In a large bowl, toss the arrugala and spinach with the Warm Cider Dressing, then season with salt and pepper. Yes, even salads should be seasoned before they are served to the customer!

Arrange on 4 salad plates, piled high. Top with the shaved red onions, split evenly amongst the plates.

Arrange the tomato halves and the gouda croutons around the edges of the plate, and top with the bacon and shaved carrots.

Tomato-Mozzarella Salad

Tomato-Mozzarella Salad is one that you will find at many restaurants. The key to a good salad is the ingredients. I will only use vine-ripened tomatoes. They always have a deeper, richer flavor than hot house tomatoes. You can see the difference right away in the color. Vine-ripened tomatoes will have a deep red color to them, and they will actually smell like tomatoes. Hot house tomatoes are typically lighter in color and hard to the touch.

1 cup	field greens, (mesclun mix)
2 T	Balsamic Dressing (page 29)
1 ea	large vine-ripened red tomato, sliced ¼" thick
1 ea	large vine-ripened yellow tomato, sliced ¼" thick
2-4 oz	fresh mozzarella balls, sliced ¼" thick
2 T	red onions, shaved
TT	kosher salt
TT	black pepper, coarse grind
2 oz	balsamic glaze*

Yield: 2 portions

Mix the field greens with the dressing, and divide over 2 plates. Season tomatoes and mozzarella with salt and pepper. Stack the tomatoes and mozzarella, using one slice of red tomato, one slice of yellow tomato, and one slice of mozzarella. Then, place the stacks atop the salad greens. Sprinkle shaved red onions evenly over the plate. Drizzle 1-2 teaspoons of the balsamic glaze over the entire dish.

*Balsamic Glaze

1 pt	balsamic vinegar
3 T	light brown sugar

Combine sugar and vinegar, reduce over a medium heat to 1/3 cup. Cool, and serve when needed.

Raviolis

Raviolis are pasta pockets filled with meats, seafood, vegetables, or poultry. They are used as an appetizer, main course, or as an accompaniment to the main dish. Raviolis can also be made with sweet fillings and used as desserts. The possibilities are endless.

At Keon's, we like to make everything possible in-house. However, when it comes to making raviolis, we will usually purchase the pasta sheets from a local vendor and make our own fillings. I don't see the need to make fresh pasta when there are so many good sources locally. It is the filling that makes the dish.

When you purchase pasta sheets from a local vendor, ask him to roll it a bit thinner than he would for lasagna. If the pasta sheets are too thick, it will give the finished product a tough texture that is undesirable. The best way to determine the best thickness is through trial and error. If you let your pasta vendor know you are making raviolis and not lasagna, he/she should get you what you need.

Once you have made your own raviolis, you will find that they are fun to make and satisfying to eat.

At Keon's, we typically make our raviolis by cutting circles or squares out of the pasta sheets. Then, we place some filling in the center, brush the edges with egg wash, and fold the pasta in half, placing the edges onto each other. We then seal the edges using a fork and crimp the sides together.

I recommend you use a store-bought template that is available at any kitchen store or online. Follow the instructions that come with the particular model you have purchased.

Ravioli templates can be found at most of your local kitchen stores: Crate and Barrel, Williams-Sonoma, etc.

Butternut Squash Raviolis

This is a nice side dish I like to serve in the fall with a brown butter sauce or an herbed, mascarpone cheese sauce. It goes well with chicken, shrimp, salmon, and a variety of other proteins. If you want to fry the raviolis, I suggest you serve them with Maple-Yogurt Dipping Sauce (page 56).

1 lb	fresh pasta sheets, thin for raviolis

Filling

1 T	vegetable oil
2 T	butter, unsalted, melted
2 T	honey
½ tsp	kosher salt
¼ tsp	black pepper, coarse grind
1 large	butternut squash, cut in half, seeds removed
½ cup	mascarpone cheese
2 ea	whole eggs
1 tsp	kosher salt
½ tsp	black pepper, coarse grind
¼ tsp	nutmeg, ground
½ cup	amaretti cookies, ground
½ cup	panko breadcrumbs

Yield: Approximately 20 large raviolis

In a small sauté pan, heat the oil, butter, honey, salt, and pepper until warm.

Score the flesh of the squash with a small knife, and brush with the honey mixture. Pour the extra honey over the squash.

Bake at 350 degrees until you can poke the squash with a fork with little resistance. This will take approximately 30 minutes. Remove from oven, and allow to cool.

Use a spoon to scrape the flesh from the skin and discard the skin. Place the flesh in a food processor, and purée until smooth.

In a bowl, mix the puréed squash with the mascarpone, eggs, salt, pepper, nutmeg, amaretti cookies, and breadcrumbs. Check the seasoning, and adjust to taste.

Using a ravioli template, fill the ravioli pockets approximately ¾ of the way. Brush with egg, and top with the second layer of pasta. Using a rolling pin, seal the raviolis as directed on the ravioli template package.

Boil in salted water for approximately 3-4 minutes. If the pasta is too thick, they may take longer.

For Fried Raviolis

Do not boil the raviolis. Instead, use a standard breading procedure, and fry in a 350-degree oil until brown.

Chestnut Raviolis

I like to use these as a seasonal dish. They are a good accompaniment with pan seared chicken, rack of lamb, and roasted pork. Their sweetness offers a nice balance to many dishes. We serve them at Keon's with the pan seared game hen and a hazelnut cream or brown butter sauce.

1 lb	fresh pasta sheets, thin for raviolis
As needed	egg wash

Filling

1 lb	chestnuts, frozen, peeled
3 oz	heavy cream
1/2 tsp	kosher salt
1/4 tsp	black pepper, coarse grind
1 ea	whole egg

Yield: Approximately 20 large raviolis

Put the chestnuts, cream, salt and pepper in a food processor; purée until smooth. Remove, and place in a bowl. Mix in the egg until thoroughly mixed. Do not add the egg to the food processor, as this may create more air and cause rupturing of the raviolis when cooking.

Using a ravioli template, fill the pockets approximately 3/4 of the way, brush with egg, and top with the second layer of pasta. Using a rolling pin, seal the raviolis as directed on the ravioli template package.

Boil in salted water for approximately 3-4 minutes. If the pasta is too thick, they may take longer.

For Fried Raviolis

Do not boil the raviolis. Instead, use a standard breading procedure, and fry in a 350-degree oil until brown.

Lemon Crusted Swordfish with Butternut Risotto and Sweet Potato Chips

Page 162

This dish is another example of how color, texture, and flavor combine to excite the palate. The initial bite is that of the crisp, lemony-flavored swordfish. Lemon always causes the mouth to water, awakening the palate. The rich creamy texture of the risotto offers a nice finish to the bite. Follow this up with a couple of salty, sweet potato chips, and you'll have a home run!

Osso Buco

Page 166

When prepared correctly, a knife is unnecessary. The meat should be tender, juicy and delectable. I like to serve this atop Whipped Yukon Potatoes or with a Butternut Squash Risotto, as shown.

Surf, Surf, and Turf

Page 172

The combination of lobster, crab cakes and filet mignon covered with just the right amount of Tomato-Basil Hollandaise is incredible! Throw in a crispy potato galette and grilled asparagus, and you've got a winning combination.

Pan Seared Game Hen with Chestnut Raviolis and Hazelnut Cream

Page 164

The key to making this a success is to be sure to have the skin golden brown and crispy. As I have mentioned numerous times throughout the book, be sure that the pan is very hot before adding the game hen to the pan. The combination of the raviolis with the sauce is incredible. Give this one a try as soon as you can. Get the game hens at a butcher who will bone them out for you to save time and aggravation.

Pan Seared Halibut
with Root Vegetable Chips

Page 179

With this dish, we are mixing flavors, colors, and textures to create a meal that pleases the eye as well as the palate. The creaminess of a risotto, combined with the salty flavor of the chips, is a winner every time!

Grilled Tenderloin Tips
with Wild Mushroom Raviolis

Page 158

An endless array of side dishes will tastefully accompany Tenderloin Tips. Mix and match side dishes according to the season, the menu or your personal preference. This dish is sure to please!

Three Brothers

Page 174

I have been serving this dish for over twenty years, and it has been a hit wherever I go. It offers the guest the opportunity to dine on multiple proteins that blend well together. The Lemon-Basil Supreme Sauce is one that compliments all aspects of the dish. If you are looking to really impress your guests, here is the recipe!

Filet Mignon with Port Wine Demi Glace

Page 152

This is a staple item at Keon's. It's a simple dish that is complimented by an outstanding sauce. Be sure to prepare the Demi Glace in advance.

It has been on the menu for years and will stay on the menu for this reason: filet done to your personal taste, combined with this exceptional sauce, is the beef lover's delight.

Grilled Pork Tenderloin with Risotto and Arrugala-Peach Salad

Page 154

This is a great fall dish when the peaches are just being harvested. The sweetness of the peaches, blended with the peppery arrugala, gives your taste buds a jolt of flavor.

Pan Seared Salmon
with Roasted Yukon Potatoes
and Cilantro-Lime Glaze

Page 176

Seen here, the Pan Seared Salmon is served with Roasted Yukon Potatoes and Ratatouille. This side dish makes another excellent seasonal accompaniment.

Blueberry Cobbler

Page 198

There's nothing tastier than a warm cobbler, with or without a scoop of ice cream. This recipe is easily modified by substituting other fruits, such as apples, peaches, apricots or nectarines.

Never Fail Crème Brûlée

Page 202

Crème Brûlée is a classic dessert that is enjoyed year-round. I like to serve mine with a fresh fruit garnish.

Chocolate Chip Bread Pudding

Page 200

All bread puddings are basic custards. Flavorings vary from recipe-to-recipe. Experiment with a variety of cereals, croissants, and breads; fruits like blueberries, or chocolate chips, to change it up a bit.

Properly seared scallops ↗   ↘ Nick and Sean

Nick Gallo and Sean Demers
enjoying the fruits of their labor!

Keon's Kitchen

Four Cheese Raviolis

These are a basic cheese ravioli, but what cookbook that has ravioli recipes would be complete without a cheese ravioli recipe? When the raviolis are fried and served with our Fra Diavolo Sauce, they are comfort food at its best!

1 lb	fresh pasta sheets, thin for raviolis

Filling

2 T	olive oil, extra virgin
1 tsp	garlic, chopped
2 T	chives, fresh, cut small
1 T	fresh parsley, chopped
1 T	fresh basil, chopped
¾ cup	ricotta cheese
¼ cup	romano cheese, grated
¼ cup	parmesan cheese, grated
¾ cup	fontina cheese, shredded
2 ea	whole eggs
½ tsp	kosher salt
½ tsp	black pepper, coarse grind

Yield: Approximately 20 large raviolis

In a large bowl, mix all the ingredients well. Check seasoning, and add salt and pepper if necessary.

Using a ravioli template, fill the pockets approximately ¾ of the way, brush with egg, and top with the second layer of pasta. Using a rolling pin, seal the raviolis as directed on the ravioli template package.

Boil in salted water for approximately 3-4 minutes. If the pasta is too thick, they may take longer.

Grilled Corn and Mascarpone Raviolis

These raviolis are extremely versatile. They make a great appetizer, an accompaniment for an entrée, the main feature of an entrée, or fried as a snack with our Maple-Yogurt Dipping Sauce.

I have served these raviolis with grilled shrimp as an appetizer, with blackened shrimp as an entrée, and topped with shrimp scampi. The options are endless!

Try them as a side dish with grilled lamb loin or all by themselves with fresh vegetables as a vegetarian option. Just be careful the pasta is thin enough to create a ravioli that is succulent, without being too thick.

These raviolis are best when served with brown butter, salt, and pepper.

1 lb	fresh pasta sheets, thin for raviolis

Filling

³⁄₄ cup	Grilled Corn (page 184)
¹⁄₂ cup	mascarpone cheese
1 ea	whole egg, shell removed
1 tsp	fresh basil
¹⁄₄ tsp	kosher salt
pinch	black pepper, coarse grind

Yield: Approximately 20 large raviolis

Mix all the ingredients in a bowl and chill.

Using a ravioli template, fill the pockets approximately ¾ of the way, brush with egg, and top with the second layer of pasta. Using a rolling pin, seal the raviolis as directed on the ravioli template package.

Boil in salted water for approximately 3-4 minutes. If the pasta is too thick, they may take longer.

For Fried Raviolis

Do not boil the raviolis. Instead, use a standard breading procedure, and fry in a 350-degree oil.

Shrimp and Scallion Raviolis

I like to serve these as an appetizer with Brown Butter Sauce (page 31). Other sauces that will compliment this dish are: alfredo, pesto, Hollandaise, and red or yellow pepper coulis.

1 lb	fresh pasta sheets, thin for raviolis

Filling

1 T	olive oil
1 T	butter, unsalted
1 tsp	garlic, chopped
1 lb	shrimp, peeled and deveined, chopped into ½" pieces
¼ cup	scallions, cut small
¼ tsp	kosher salt
¼ tsp	black pepper, coarse grind
¼ tsp	Old Bay® Seasoning
¾ cup	ricotta cheese
2 ea	whole eggs
pinch	kosher salt
pinch	black pepper, coarse grind

Yield: Approximately 20 large raviolis

In a medium-sized sauté pan, heat the oil and butter over medium-high heat. Add the garlic, and stir for 30 seconds. DO NOT BROWN. Add the chopped shrimp and toss to evenly distribute the garlic. Cook for three minutes or until the shrimp, are cooked. Do not over cook as this will make the shrimp tough.

Season with salt, pepper, and Old Bay Seasoning. Remove from the heat, and allow to cool.

In a bowl, combine the cooked shrimp with the ricotta and eggs, season to taste.

Using a ravioli template, fill the pockets approximately ¾ of the way, brush with egg, and top with the second layer of pasta. Using a rolling pin, seal the raviolis as directed on the ravioli template package.

Boil in salted water for approximately 3-4 minutes. If the pasta is too thick, they may take longer.

For Fried Raviolis

Do not boil the raviolis. Instead, use a standard breading procedure, and fry in a 350-degree oil until brown.

Spinach and Goat Cheese Raviolis

These raviolis can be matched with a variety of dishes. They go well with poultry dishes, steak tips, pork, and a variety of seafood dishes.

They can also be used as an appetizer, topped with a sun dried tomato coulis, a light cream sauce, or a Brown Butter Sauce. If you like fried raviolis, these are the best.

1 lb	fresh pasta sheets, thin for raviolis

Filling

1 T	butter, unsalted
2 cups	fresh baby spinach, firmly packed
1/4 tsp	kosher salt
1/4 tsp	black pepper, course grind
1/4 cup	mascarpone cheese
1/4 cup	goat cheese, chevre
1 ea	whole egg
1 ea	egg yolk
pinch	ground allspice
pinch	kosher salt
pinch	black pepper, coarse grind

Yield: Approximately 20 large raviolis

In a medium-sized sauté pan, melt the butter over medium-high heat. Add the spinach, a pinch of salt and pepper, and toss until wilted. Remove from the pan and chill. Once chilled, chop the spinach small, then add the rest of the ingredients, and mix well.

Using a ravioli template, fill the pockets approximately ¾ of the way, brush with egg, and top with the second layer of pasta. Using a rolling pin, seal the raviolis as directed on the ravioli template package.

Boil in salted water for approximately 3-4 minutes. If the pasta is too thick, they may take longer.

For Fried Raviolis

Do not boil the raviolis. Instead, use a standard breading procedure, and fry in a 350-degree oil until brown.

Sun Dried Tomato-Basil Raviolis

These are one of my favorite raviolis. They go great with a variety of dishes.

They are a delicious appetizer when served with wilted spinach and a brown butter sauce. When fried and served with our Lemon-Basil Supreme Sauce, they are a good way to begin any meal. I like to use these as a side to accompany a pan seared halibut or sea bass. When tossed with chicken and summer vegetables, you have a well-balanced meal full of flavor and color.

1 lb	fresh pasta sheets, thin for raviolis

Filling

1 T	butter, unsalted
$1/2$ cup	red onion, $1/4$" dice
$3/4$ cups	sun dried tomatoes, good quality, $1/4$" dice
1 tsp	garlic, chopped
$1/4$ tsp	black pepper, coarse grind
$1/2$ cup	mascarpone cheese
$1/2$ cup	goat cheese, chevre
$3/4$ cup	ricotta cheese
1 ea	whole egg
1 ea	egg yolk
3 T	basil, fresh, chopped
$1/4$ cup	panko breadcrumbs
pinch	kosher salt
pinch	black pepper, coarse grind

Yield: Approximately 20 large raviolis

In a medium-sized sauté pan, melt the butter over medium-high heat. Add the red onions, and sweat until translucent. Add the sun dried tomatoes, and cook over medium heat for about 3-4 minutes. Add the garlic, and stir constantly for 1 minute so the garlic does not brown. Add the black pepper, and remove from heat. Let cool.

In a separate bowl, mix all the remaining ingredients, and fold in the sun dried tomato mixture.

Using a ravioli template, fill the pockets approximately ¾ of the way, brush with egg, and top with the second layer of pasta. Using a rolling pin, seal the raviolis as directed on the ravioli template package.

Boil in salted water for approximately 3-4 minutes. If the pasta is too thick, they may take longer.

For Fried Raviolis

Do not boil the raviolis. Instead, use a standard breading procedure, and fry in a 350-degree oil.

Wild Mushroom Raviolis

These raviolis also can be matched with a variety of dishes. They go well with poultry dishes, steak tips, pork, and a variety of seafood dishes. These are also good fried and served with Fra Diavolo Sauce.

1 lb	fresh pasta sheets, thin for raviolis

Filling

2 T	butter, unsalted
3 ea	shallots, chopped
1 T	garlic, chopped
1 cup	shiitake mushrooms, chopped small
1 cup	oyster mushrooms, chopped small
1 cup	portabella mushrooms, chopped small
1/2 tsp	kosher salt
1/2 tsp	black pepper, coarse grind
1/2 tsp	fresh thyme leaves
1 tsp	chives, fresh, chopped
1/2 cup	ricotta cheese
1/4 cup	goat cheese, chevre
1/3 cup	panko breadcrumbs
2 ea	whole eggs

Yield: Approximately 20 large raviolis

In a 4-quart saucepot, melt the butter over medium-high heat. Add the shallots, and stir until translucent.

Add the garlic, and continue to stir for 30 seconds. Add the mushrooms, and cook for 7 minutes over high heat, stirring occasionally. Stir in the salt, pepper, thyme leaves and chives, and remove from heat.

Place the cooked mushroom mixture into a sieve using a ladle. Put pressure on the mushrooms to drain the liquid. Reduce the liquid by ½ add it back to the mushrooms, and cool.

Add the cheeses, breadcrumbs and eggs, and mix well.

Using a ravioli template, fill the pockets approximately ¾ of the way, brush with egg, and top with the second layer of pasta. Using a rolling pin, seal the raviolis as directed on the ravioli template package.

Boil in salted water for approximately 3-4 minutes. If the pasta is too thick, they may take longer.

For Fried Raviolis

Do not boil the raviolis. Instead, use a standard breading procedure, and fry in a 350-degree oil.

Stocks

The definition of a stock is: "A liquid in which bones, vegetables and spices are cooked."

The difference between a stock and a broth is that a broth gets its flavor from the juices of the meats or poultry that was cooked. Bones are not used in the making of a broth. Therefore, its flavor will be significantly weaker.

Never substitute a broth for a stock unless you are prepared to be disappointed. The flavors of a stock are much richer in both color and flavor. The recipes that follow have been tested, and I'm sure you will be pleased with the end product to produce wonderful sauces.

Remember, always allow your stocks to simmer for the recommended time specified in the recipe. Periodically, brush the inside of the pot above the liquid to prevent a crust from forming. This crust has great flavor that you will be losing if you allow it to adhere to the inside of the pot. It also makes cleaning the pot later a whole lot easier.

Fish Stock

This makes a good stock for fish chowder, seafood chowder, or a fish sauce. It has a nice fish flavor without being too strong. You will see that I have ½ teaspoon of kosher salt in this recipe. I know that all classical stocks are made without salt. I have never agreed with this. The reasoning behind "no salt" is that when you reduce stock to enhance its flavor, it will become salty. That is why I only use a small amount. I use just enough to give the stock better taste without over seasoning.

2 qts	cold water
1 ea	large leeks or 1 medium-sized onion
1 ea	large carrot
1 ea	celery stalk, with leaves
2 ea	bay leaves
12 ea	black peppercorns
2 ea	sprigs of thyme
4 ea	parsley stems
½ ea	lemon
1½ lbs	fish bones
½ tsp	kosher salt

Yield: ½ gallon

Combine all ingredients in an 8-quart saucepot. Bring to a boil, and immediately reduce to a simmer. Simmer for 45 minutes, and strain. Taste the stock. If you want it to be a bit stronger, strain it and reduce by ¼.

Roasted Chicken Stock

This chicken stock will be rich in flavor and have a deep color when done correctly.

5 lbs	chicken parts, backs, necks, wings
5 qts	water, cold
1 ea	large onion
2 ea	large carrot
4 ea	celery stalks
3 ea	bay leaves
8 ea	sprigs of parsley
15 ea	black peppercorns
2 ea	sprigs of thyme
1 tsp	kosher salt

Yield: 3 quarts

Spread the chicken parts out on a sheet pan, and bake at 375 degrees for about 30 minutes, or until golden brown. Transfer the bones to a pot with all other ingredients. Deglaze the sheet pan with some of the water, and then add the liquid to the cooking pot.

Bring this to a boil, and reduce to a simmer. Be sure all the ingredients are submerged during cooking. I like to place a small cooling rack on top of the pot to keep everything submerged. Simmer for 3 1/2 hours. Add water if the level of water goes below the bones. Strain the stock. Cool quickly and refrigerate. Taste the stock. If it is weak, strain it and reduce by 1/4.

Veal Stock

This veal stock will be rich in flavor and have a deep color when done correctly. The key to making a very good veal stock is in the caramelizing of the vegetables and bones. See photo on page 42. The darker you get the vegetables and bones, without burning them, the richer and stronger your stock will come out.

Again, don't take short cuts. Take your time, the end result will be well worth it.

10 lbs	veal bones, 2" long (marrow bones are best)
10 oz	tomato paste
3 T	vegetable oil
2 ea	large onions, cut 1 ½" dice
4 ea	large carrot, ½" slices
8 ea	celery stalks, ½" slices
5 oz	tomato paste
10 qts	water, cold
6 ea	bay leaves
16 ea	sprigs of parsley
4 ea	garlic cloves
3 T	black peppercorns
6 ea	sprigs of thyme
2 tsp	kosher salt

Yield: 3 quarts

Spread the veal bones out on a sheet pan, and bake at 475 degrees for 45 minutes–1 hour, or until deep brown. Smear the 10 oz paste on the bones evenly, and return to the oven for additional 25 minutes, or until the tomato paste is *beginning* to blacken. DO NOT BURN.

In a large, wide rimmed pot, heat the oil until very hot, and add the onions. Sauté for 10 minutes, stirring occasionally, until the onions are beginning to brown. Add the celery and carrots, and continue to brown slowly over medium heat. This should take 35-45 minutes.

Once the vegetables are nicely caramelized, add the 5 oz tomato paste, and reduce heat to low. Stir until all vegetables are evenly coated with the paste. Continue to cook the vegetables and tomato paste over low heat to get a darker color. Once the vegetables are dark, deglaze the pot with 1/2 cup of the cold water, and stir thoroughly with a wooden spoon, scraping the bottom to avoid burning. Continue to cook over medium heat, stirring occasionally, until all the liquid has evaporated, and the vegetables are even darker than before. Then deglaze with a gallon of water, and be sure all of the product is loosened from the pot. The entire process should take 45 minutes to 1 hour.

Transfer the bones and the vegetables to a 24-quart pot with all other ingredients. Deglaze the sheet pan with some of the water from the recipe above, and add the liquid to the cooking pot.

Bring this to a boil, and reduce to a simmer. Be sure that all the ingredients are submerged during cooking. I like to place a small cooling rack on top of the pot to keep everything submerged. Simmer for 5 1/2 hours, adding a cup of water occasionally to be sure everything is constantly submerged. Brush the sides of the pot with some of the stock occasionally. The crust that forms on the sides of the pot is full of flavor, don't waste it! Strain the stock. Reduce it by 1/2 by simmering. Cool quickly and refrigerate.

A remoulage is the second wetting of the bones. In other words, a second, somewhat weaker stock. For this, take the used bones, add a new set of the ingredients above, and simmer for 4 hours. No roasting is necessary for a remoulage. Strain and cool. This second stock is weaker, but will still have good flavor for soups and sauces if reduced enough. I like to reduce my remoulage by 1/2 after it has been strained.

Keon's Kitchen – Secret Recipes from the Award-Winning Restaurant

Main Courses

The main course recipes I have given you in this book all have a protein, starch, and vegetable of some sort. This is the classic style of entrée presentation.

Our plating styles have changed from the old "10 o'clock, 2 o'clock, 6 o'clock" style. This means if the plate were the face of a clock, the starch goes on the plate at 10 o'clock, the vegetable at 2 o'clock, and the proteins at 6 o'clock. I find this style to be boring and outdated. Stack your food, layer it, give it style, color, and panache!

And don't forget to garnish your food. This is the finishing touch. Use flavored oils for color. Chopped herbs, vegetables, or a lettuce, like radicchio, make flavorful and colorful garnishes. Even a sauce squirted neatly out of a squirt bottle can be seen as a creative way to garnish your plates. Whatever you do, have fun!

Cider Glazed Pork Chops

This has been a staple at Keon's since the previous owner, Michael Keon, opened its doors in the late 1990's. Some minor alterations have been made through the years. But, this is a recipe that is sure to please. It is important to soak the pork chops in a brine for 48 hours for the best results. A brine is a liquid with a very high salt content.

It is used to preserve, pickle, and flavor food items. I call for "frenched pork chops." What I mean is the pork chop bone should be clean and free of any sinew or fat. Your butcher can do this for you. The cider glaze should be made ahead of time.

For the Brine

1/3 cup	kosher salt
1/3 cup	brown sugar
¼ cup	pickling spice
½ gallon	cold water
4 ea	14 oz pork chops, frenched
2 T	canola oil
TT	kosher salt
TT	black pepper, coarse grind
8 oz	Cider Glaze*
6 oz	Roasted Chicken Stock or broth
4 T	butter, unsalted
20 oz	Whipped Yukon Potatoes (page 194)
12 oz	baby carrots, blanched, heated in butter

Yield: 4 portions

Mix the ingredients for the brine, and soak the 4 chops for 48 hours. Then remove chops from the brine, and discard the brine. Coat the pork chops with the canola oil, and season with the salt and pepper. Put on a very hot and clean grill. Cook for 3 minutes, giving the meat the proper grill lines and turn over. Cook for 2 minutes, and then remove the chops from the grill. Divide them into 2 hot skillets with ½ of the cider glaze and the Roasted Chicken Stock already simmering in each pan. Place the skillet on the bottom of a 450-degree oven for approximately 10 minutes. Turn the chops over, and be sure the sauce has not completely evaporated. If you need more liquid, add a little Chicken Stock. Cook until you have reached your desired cook temperature. I like to serve our chops at medium (140 degrees internal temp). This usually takes 12–15 minutes.

Remove the chop from the pan, and if the sauce is loose, reduce it by simmering, until it is thick enough to coat the back of a wooden spoon. Once the desired thickness is obtained, whisk in the butter and check the seasoning.

Place ¼ of the Whipped Yukon Potatoes on each of the 4 plates. Lean a chop against the potatoes with the bone straight up. Arrange the baby carrots on each of the plates, and nape' the sauce over the chops.

*Cider Glaze Reduction

½ gallon	apple cider, fresh (apple juice is NOT a good substitute)
14 oz	tomato juice

Combine and reduce to 1 pint. This should be the thickness of cream. It can be made ahead and kept refrigerated for up to 2 weeks.

Coq Au Vin

This is a classic French dish. Most of the dishes served at Keon's have a classic French foundation. This dis is no different. The process takes a while, but the finished product is well worth the effort.

¼ cup	canola oil for browning
4 ea	whole leg quarters
2 ea	large carrots
1 ea	medium yellow onion
4 ea	celery stalks
1 lb	button mushrooms, quartered
1 cup	burgundy wine
½ tsp	kosher salt
½ tsp	black pepper, coarse grind
3 ea	fresh thyme, sprigs
3 ea	bay leaves
5 ea	parsley sprigs
3 qts	Roasted Chicken Stock, previously prepared (page 143)
½ cup	tomatoes, chopped
3 oz	butter, softened
3 oz	flour

Yield: 4 portions

Heat the oil in a large rondo (wide stock pot) until it is almost smoking.

Add the chicken legs, brown on all sides and remove from the pan. Add the carrots, celery, and onions, and reduce the heat to medium, stirring occasionally. Once the vegetables are lightly browned, add the mushrooms, and sauté 2 minutes. Add the wine, and reduce by ½.

Put the chicken legs back in the pan, add the rest of the ingredients and bring to a simmer. Cover, and place in a 350-degree oven for 3 hours. Gently remove the chicken and vegetables from the stock. Discard the bay leaves, thyme, and parsley.

Mix the flour and butter together to make the uncooked roux.

Add the uncooked roux to the stock while whisking vigorously. Check the seasoning, and add salt and pepper if necessary.

I like to serve the Coq Au Vin with Whipped Yukon Potatoes along with the carrots and celery from the cooking liquid.

Filet Mignon with Port Wine Demi Glace

This is a staple item at Keon's. It has been on the menu for years and will stay on the menu. It is a simple dish that is complimented by an outstanding sauce. The sauce can and should be made in advance. Have the Whipped Yukon Potatoes done and held warm.

1 T	canola oil
2 ea	8 oz filet mignons
TT	kosher salt
TT	black pepper, coarse grind
10 oz	Whipped Yukon Potatoes (page 194)
10 ea	Grilled Asparagus Spears (page 183)
4 oz	Port Wine Demi Glace, see below*

Yield: 2 portions

Heat the canola oil in a small sauté pan over high heat. Once the pan is smoking hot, add the filets, and allow them to get a good sear. This should take about 3 minutes. Turn the filets over in the pan and place in a 400-degree oven until they are just below the desired cook temperature. (See temperature chart on page 16).

When the steaks are cooked, remove them from the oven, and let them rest for 5 minutes.

Plating

Place ½ of the Whipped Yukon Potatoes in the center of each of 2 plates. Lean the filet against the potatoes, and napé the sauce over the filet. Lean the Grilled Asparagus next to the filet (as shown on page 120).

*Port Wine Demi Glace

A classical demi glace is ½ veal stock and ½ veal sauce reduced by half.

Here is how we do it at Keon's.

Take 1 quart of port wine, and reduce it to 1 cup.

Follow the recipe for Veal Stock (page 144), and combine it with the reduced port wine. Bring this to a simmer, and reduce the sauce to 1 ½ quarts.

This sauce is a reduction sauce and nothing more. We do not use a thickening agent of any kind.

Grilled Pork Tenderloin
with Arrugala and Peaches

This is a great fall dish when the peaches are just being harvested. The sweetness of the peaches, blended with the peppery arrugala, gives your taste buds a jolt of flavor. Be sure to have the risotto cooking when you grill the tenderloin

1 T	canola oil
2 ea	pork tenderloins, 10-12 oz
TT	kosher salt
TT	black pepper, coarse grind
12 oz	Lemon Pepper Risotto (page 193)
4 oz	baby arrugala
1 ea	fresh peach, peeled and sliced
1 oz	Honey-Champagne Vinaigrette (page 55)
TT	kosher salt
TT	black pepper, coarse grind
1 tsp	chives, chopped

Yield: 2 portions

Rub the pork tenderloins with the canola oil, and season them with the salt and pepper. Place the tenderloins on a clean, hot grill. Grill to the desired temperature.

Plating

Place ½ of the Lemon Pepper Risotto in the center of two plates. Slice the tenderloin as shown in the photo on page 121.

In a small bowl, toss the baby arrugala, peaches, Honey-Champagne Vinaigrette, and seasoning.

Place this atop the tenderloin as shown in photo.

Lemon-Pepper Risotto

Follow the recipe on page 192 for Sun Dried Tomato Risotto, but omit the sun dried tomatoes.

Add 1 tsp of lemon zest and ½ tsp of black pepper at the beginning of the cooking process.

Grilled Rib Eye with Blue Cheese, Whipped Yukon Potatoes and Cipollini Onion Gravy

This is a meat lovers dream. Who could ask for better than a 14 oz rib eye smothered in a cipollini onion gravy along with whipped potatoes, with just a hint of blue cheese to give it a boost, and haricots vert (green beans). My mouth is watering as I write this. As a matter of fact, I think I'll take a break now and go throw this dish together....Okay I'm back! Below is the recipe for your dining pleasure, bon appétit!

2 ea	14 oz rib eye steaks, allowed to rest at room temperature for ½ hour
2 T	canola oil
TT	kosher salt
TT	black pepper, coarse grind
6 oz	Cipollini Onion Gravy, previously prepared (page 49)
12 oz	Whipped Yukon Potatoes (page 194)
1 oz	blue cheese, a soft variety like gorgonzola works best
6 oz	haricots vert
1 T	butter

Yield: 2 portions

Have the whipped potatoes ready, and warm before grilling the rib eye. Also have the Cipollini Onion Gravy working and close to finished, so that you can keep an eye on the steaks as they are cooking.

The haricots vert should be snipped and blanched in a small sauté pan with the butter on the stove, but without heat. We'll heat them at the last minute.

Rub the rib eyes with the canola oil, salt and pepper. Place them on a clean, hot grill. Cook for 2 minutes, and turn the steak at an angle to give it diamond-shaped grill marks. Cook for an additional 2 minutes, and turn the steak over. Cook to desired temperature. Remove from the grill, and allow to rest for 5-10 minutes near the stove.

While the steak is resting, put a medium heat under the haricots vert and season with salt and pepper.

Place a mound of potatoes on the center of the plate and place the steak on top of the potatoes to give height to the plate. Napé with the Cipollini Onion Gravy, and use the haricots vert as a garnish.

Grilled Tenderloin Tips
with Wild Mushroom Raviolis

It is what it is! This dish is sure to please. Remember to let the steak tips rest after grilling (see rest/resting in the glossary).

2 T	canola oil
TT	kosher salt
TT	black pepper, coarse grind
24 oz	tenderloin tips
½ gallon	boiling water
1 T	kosher salt
16 ea	Wild Mushroom Raviolis (page 138)
2 T	butter
TT	kosher salt
TT	black pepper, coarse grind
3 oz	Demi Glace, hot
1 T	chopped chives

Yield: 2 portions

Put the canola oil, salt and pepper in a medium-sized bowl, and add the tips. Mix well so that all of the tips are seasoned and coated with oil. Allow to rest at room temperature for 30 minutes.

Place the tips on the grill, and grill to just <u>less</u> than your desired temperature. For instance, if you like your tips medium rare, remove them from the grill at rare-medium rare. Allow to rest for 5 minutes.

While the meat is resting, put the raviolis in the boiling, salted water, and cook the raviolis until they are "al dente." This should only take 3 minutes or so, depending on the thickness of the pasta. While the raviolis are boiling, melt the butter in a large skillet. When the raviolis are done, add them to the skillet, and toss with salt and pepper. Place half of the raviolis on each of 2 plates.

In a bowl, mix the hot Demi Glace with the tenderloin tips, and place atop the raviolis. Garnish with chopped chives.

Korean BBQ Pork

This is one of those dishes that has evolved through the years. The recipe changes slightly as we go on. I'm not sure there are even any ingredients that would make this dish Korean, but who cares? My guests love it, and I'm pretty sure there would be a rebellion in the streets if I took it off the menu. Again, this is an item that takes a long time to cook, but the prep time is fairly short.

5 lbs	pork butt
2 ea	medium yellow onions, quartered
6 ea	bay leaves
16 ea	black peppercorns
As needed	cold water

For the sauce

2 ¼ cups	cider vinegar
2 ea	bay leaves
3 ea	cloves of garlic
1 cup	dark brown sugar
2/3 cup	soy sauce
1 tsp	cinnamon, ground
1 tsp	cumin, ground
1 tsp	allspice, ground
½ tsp	black pepper, coarse grind
12 oz	tomato paste
All remaining	braising liquid, reduced by half (after reduction, you should have approx. 2 cups)

Yield: 12 portions

In a wide-rimmed pot, place the pork butt, quartered yellow onions, bay leaves, peppercorns, and enough cold water to cover the pork. Bring this to a boil, and place in a 350-degree oven for 3-4 hours. It is ready when the bone comes away from the meat easily.

Once the pork is cooked, remove it from the liquid along with the peppercorns, bay leaves and onions. Reduce the cooking liquid by 1/2 over medium-high heat.

Combine all of the second set of ingredients in the cooking pot along with the cooked pork butt. Simmer over a low heat for 3 hours, stirring occasionally. Be careful not to let it stick to the bottom of the pot. It is done when you have a nice, thick sauce, and all of the meat is broken apart and tender. Serve with Yukon Potato Chips and Aioli.

Lemon Crusted Swordfish with Butternut Risotto and Sweet Potato Chips

Blending textures and flavors is something I have preached throughout this book. This dish is another example of how color, texture, and flavor combine to excite the palate.

The initial bite is that of a crisp, lemony-flavored, swordfish and the sweet creaminess of the risotto.

Lemon always causes the mouth to water, awakening the palate. The rich creamy texture of the risotto offers a nice finish to the bite. Follow this up with a couple of salty, sweet potato chips, and you have a meal that is sure to please.

1 ea	sweet potato, peeled, sliced paper thin
As needed	oil for frying

Coating

1 cup	panko breadcrumbs
1 T	fresh lemon rind
¼ tsp	cayenne pepper
1 T	lemon juice
TT	kosher salt
TT	black pepper, coarse grind
2 ea	8 oz swordfish steaks, skin & blood line removed, 1" thick
2 T	canola oil
1 ½ cups	Butternut Risotto (page 193)
1 T	chives, chopped

Yield: 2 portions

Take the sweet potato slices, and fry in a 300-degree fryer until brown and crispy. Remove, and place on paper towels or papyrus plates to absorb the excess fat. Salt liberally. These chips should be done ahead of time

Combine the breadcrumbs, cayenne, and lemon rind in a food processor, and run on high for 5 seconds, no longer. Put this in an 8"x 8" pan or something that will keep the breadcrumbs from making a mess when you coat the swordfish.

Evenly coat the swordfish with lemon juice, and season with salt and pepper. Place the swordfish in the breadcrumb mixture and press down hard to get a good coating on the fish. Turn the fish over, and repeat the process.

Begin the risotto, and when it is about half-cooked, heat the 2 T of canola oil in a skillet until it is almost smoking. Add the swordfish and brown. Turn the fish over, and brown it on the second side. This will only take 1 minute or so on each side. Be careful not to burn. Once the swordfish is browned on both sides, place them in a 350-degree oven for 4-5 minutes. The swordfish should have an internal temperature of 145 degrees when done.

Plating

Split the risotto onto 2 plates, and place the swordfish on top of the rice. Take a handful of sweet potato chips, and pile them on top of the fish.

Pan Seared Game Hen with Chestnut Raviolis and Hazelnut Cream

The key to making this a success is to be sure to have the skin golden brown and crispy. As I have mentioned numerous times throughout the book, be sure that the pan is very hot before adding the game hen to the pan. The combination of the raviolis with the sauce is incredible. Give this dish a try as soon as you can. Get the game hens from a butcher who will bone them out for you to save time and aggravation. Start the hazelnut cream first so that is has enough time to finish before the game hen.

2 T	canola oil
2 ea	20-24 oz game hens, boned out (12 - 14 oz after bones are removed)
TT	kosher salt
TT	black pepper, coarse grind
½ gallon	boiling water
12 ea	large Chestnut Raviolis, previously prepared (page 112)
2 T	butter, unsalted
TT	kosher salt
TT	black pepper, coarse grind

Hazelnut Cream Sauce

1 T	butter, unsalted
2 T	shallots, chopped
¼ cup	toasted hazelnuts, chopped quickly in a food processor so they are small pieces
½ cup	Roasted Chicken Stock, previously prepared (page 143)
¼ cup	heavy cream

TT	kosher salt
TT	black pepper, coarse grind
5 oz	haricots vert, cooked, seasoned and warm

Yield: 2 portions

For the Hazelnut Cream Sauce

Heat the butter in a small sauce pot. Add the chopped shallots, and sweat until translucent. Add the hazelnuts, Roasted Chicken Stock and heavy cream. Simmer over a low heat until needed. Be sure to stir the sauce occasionally, and add Roasted Chicken Stock or cream if it seems to be getting too thick. Season with salt and pepper before serving.

For the Game Hens

Heat the oil in a skillet large enough to fit both game hens. If you do not have one large enough, use 2 separate pans. It is important the game hens can lay flat in the pan with enough surface area for browning.

Place the hens in the skillet, skin-side down. Cook until the skin is golden brown and crispy. Turn the hens over, and place the pan in a 400-degree oven for approximately 15 minutes. The time depends on the size of the game hens. Do not over cook! Use a thermometer. The internal temperature of the hens should be 160 degrees when done. Once the hens are cooked, allow to rest for 5 minutes. Cut the hens in half for plating.

While the game hens are in the oven, boil the raviolis until "al dente." This should take 3-5 minutes, depending on the thickness of the pasta. When cooked, remove from the water, drain, and toss in a pan with the butter, salt, and pepper.

Plating

Place the raviolis on the plate, and stack the game hens on top of the raviolis. Napé the sauce over the game hens, and garnish with the warm haricots verts.

Osso Buco

This is one of the most popular dishes we have here at Keon's. (after the Three Brothers, of course).

When prepared correctly, a knife is unnecessary. The meat should be tender, juicy and delectable. I like to serve this atop Whipped Yukon Potatoes or with a Butternut Squash Risotto. Although I don't mention it in the procedure, I like to pull the vegetables out and serve them along with the Osso Buco. The flavor they have is incredible, though the appearance is not the greatest.

4 ea	Osso Buco, 12-14 oz
As needed	butcher's twine
As needed	all purpose flour
¼ cup	vegetable oil
1 ea	yellow onion, large, cut into 1" chunks
4 ea	carrots, cut into 1" chunks
4 ea	celery stalks, cut into 1" chunks
1 cup	burgundy wine
2 cups	Veal Stock, previously prepared (page 144)
2 cups	water
4 ea	bay leaves
2 ea	rosemary sprigs
6 ea	thyme sprigs
½ tsp	kosher salt
¼ tsp	black pepper, coarse grind
3 T	butter, unsalted, cut into small pieces

Yield: 4 portions

First, tie the outsides of the Osso Buco to help keep them together while they cook.

In a 10-quart braising pot, heat the oil over a medium-high heat. Flour the Osso Buco lightly. When the oil is hot, brown the meat on both sides, and remove from the pot. Add the onions, carrots, and celery, and reduce heat to medium. Brown the vegetables about 20 minutes, stirring occasionally.

Deglaze with the burgundy, and simmer until the liquid is reduced by $1/2$. Add the rest of the ingredients and the meat, and bring to a boil. Cover and place in a 400-degree oven for approximately 4 hours. Check, every 45 minutes or so to be sure there is enough liquid. Do not let the liquid reduce past halfway. Add $1/2$ cup water and $1/2$ cup veal stock if necessary.

When done, check with a fork to be sure the meat is tender.

Once the meat is tender, remove it from the liquid and place it on a serving platter. Remove the twine and discard. Cover the meat with foil, and keep it in a 250-degree oven until needed. Strain the cooking liquid through a sieve, and return it to the stove. Reduce by simmering until there is approximately 2 cups remaining. Whisk in the butter. Check the seasoning, and napé some of the sauce over the meat. Serve with Whipped Yukon Potatoes (page 194) and vegetables of your choice.

Serve the rest of the sauce in a service boat.

Pan Seared Diver Scallops with Arrugala and Golden Raisin Chutney

This is a great cold weather dish. It combines the savory flavor of the arrugala and the sweet flavors of the chutney. I put this on the menu over a year ago and cannot take it off. Although, I feel that this is a perfect cold weather dish, our customers love it year-round.

Be sure the scallops you are using are dry. Place on a paper towel before cooking, if necessary.

1 ½ T	canola oil
8 ea	Diver scallops, U–10's, dry
1 cup	baby arrugala, washed, dried
3 T	Honey-Champagne Vinaigrette, previously prepared (page 55)
1 cup	Roasted Cauliflower Purée, hot (page 189)
¾ cup	Golden Raisin Chutney, warm (page 52)
2 T	Balsamic Glaze, cold (page 107)
TT	kosher salt
TT	black pepper, coarse grind

Yield: 2 portions

Heat a 12" skillet to the smoking point. Add the canola oil, and swirl it in the pan. Season the scallops with salt and pepper. Take the pan away from the stove, and carefully place the scallops, leaving a 1" space between. Let the scallops brown over high heat, and then turn them over. I like the scallops to be almost crispy brown before turning them over. This should take about 2 minutes. Place in a 400-degree oven for about 4 minutes.

Plating

In a bowl, toss the baby arrugala with the Honey-Champagne Vinaigrette. Season with salt and pepper. Spread the dressed arrugala out in a line across the plate. Spoon the Roasted Cauliflower Purée next to the arrugala in a line as well. Place 4 scallops in a row on top of the Roasted Cauliflower Purée. Spoon ½ of the Golden Raisin Chutney onto the arrugala across the top. Drizzle the Balsamic Glaze for color (see photo on page 46).

Pan Seared Lamb Loin with Spinach and Goat Cheese Raviolis

I love using lamb loin instead of a rack of lamb or a lamb leg. The reason is because lamb loins typically do not have the game meat flavor that the leg or rack may have. The white peach purée gives the breadcrumbs something to adhere to. You can get the purée on line or at PerfectPurees.com. Buy the lamb loins at your local butcher, and request he trim them for you. There should not be any fat or silver skin remaining on the loin. Once you have found the products, this dish is awesome. We like to serve this dish with Madeira Demi Glace.

TT	kosher salt
TT	black pepper, coarse grind
4 ea	7 oz lamb loins, trimmed, silver skin removed
½ cup	white peach purée
2 ea	eggs
1 ½ cups	panko breadcrumbs
¼ cup	canola oil
½ gallon	boiling water
24 ea	Spinach and Goat Cheese Raviolis (page 134)
3 T	butter, unsalted
TT	kosher salt
TT	black pepper, coarse grind
16 ea	baby carrots with 1" tops, blanched, seasoned, and heated

Madeira Demi Glace

3 oz	Madeira wine
6 oz	Demi Glace, hot (page 62)
2 T	butter, unsalted
TT	kosher salt
TT	black pepper, coarse grind

Yield: 4 portions

For the Madeira Demi Glace

Place the madeira wine in a small saucepot over medium heat, and reduce it by two-thirds.

Add the Demi Glace, and bring it to a simmer. Whisk in the butter and season with salt and pepper. Keep warm until needed.

Season the lamb loins with salt and pepper. Mix the peach purée with the 2 eggs to make an egg wash. Dip the lamb loins in the egg wash and roll in the breadcrumbs. Be sure the loins are evenly covered with breadcrumbs.

Heat the oil in a large skillet until very hot. It should have the consistency of water when it is hot enough. Fry the lamb loins until brown on all sides. Be careful, the breadcrumbs will brown quickly if the oil is hot enough. Once the lamb is browned, place in a 350-degree oven until it reaches your desired internal temperature. Remove lamb from the oven, and allow to rest for 5 minutes.

While the lamb is resting, melt the butter in a medium-sized skillet.

Place the raviolis in the boiling water, and cook them until "al dente." This should take 3-5 minutes, depending on the thickness of the pasta. Remove the raviolis from the water, and toss them in the pan with the butter. Season with salt and pepper.

Arrange 6 raviolis on each of the 4 plates. Slice the lamb diagonally, and fan across the center of the plate. Drizzle the Madeira Demi Glace over the lamb and raviolis. Garnish with the baby carrots with tops.

Surf, Surf, and Turf

This is Three Brothers extreme! The combination of lobster, crab cakes and filet mignon, covered with just the right amount of Tomato-Basil Hollandaise, is incredible! Throw in a crispy potato galette and Grilled Asparagus, and you've got a dish that is sure to please. This is one of our most popular dishes at Keon's. The key to making this dish perfect is blanching the lobster for only 5 minutes. You don't want to overcook it and ruin the dish.

¼ cup	vegetable oil
4-6 oz	filet mignons, grilled
2 ea	1 ½ lb Maine lobsters, blanched 5 minutes, claws, tails, and knuckles removed
4 ea	3 oz Texas Crab Cakes, previously prepared (page 82)
TT	kosher salt
TT	black pepper, coarse grind
2 T	butter, unsalted
8 oz	Tomato-Basil Hollandaise, previously prepared (page 54)
4 ea	Potato Galette, previously prepared (page 187)
20 ea	spears of Grilled Asparagus, medium sized
2 T	fresh basil chiffonade

Yield: 4 portions

To assemble this dish correctly, have your potato galettes cooked and in the oven when starting to cook the proteins. Have your Hollandaise and asparagus done and held warm.

Have 2 10″ sauté pans on very high heat and a 3rd sauté pan on low heat with the 2 T of butter melting.

When the sauté pans are sufficiently hot, add ½ of the oil to each of the 2 hot pans.

Season and sear the tenderloins for 2 minutes on each side. Place in a 350-degree oven for 6 minutes.

Season, and sear your crab cakes to a golden brown on each side, and place them in the same 350-degree oven for 3 minutes.

I recommend a medium filet for this particular dish. Both the filets and the crab cakes should be finished within 1 minute of each other.

Season, and add the lobster meat to the melted butter while the filets and crab cakes are in the oven. Cook over a medium-high heat until hot throughout.

Plating

Place a hot potato galette on each of 4 plates. Place a filet on each of the galettes and a crab cake on top of the filet. Top with lobster meat, evenly distributed. Napé with the Hollandaise Sauce, and garnish with basil chiffonade.

Three Brothers

I have been serving this dish for over 20 years, and it has been a hit wherever I go. It offers the guest the opportunity to dine on multiple proteins that blend well together. The Lemon-Basil Supreme Sauce is one that compliments all aspects of the dish. If you are looking to really impress your guests, here is the recipe! Be sure to read it thoroughly before starting. This can be a complicated plating for the inexperienced.

4 T	canola oil
4 ea	4 oz filets mignon
8 ea	2 oz boneless chicken breasts, pounded to ½" thick
8 ea	shrimp, peeled, deveined (U-10's)
TT	kosher salt
TT	black pepper, coarse grind
24 oz	Whipped Yukon Potatoes (page 194)
8 oz	heavy cream
3 T	lemon juice
1 T	fresh basil, chopped
TT	kosher salt
TT	black pepper, coarse grind
20 ea	asparagus spears, grilled and hot

Yield: 4 portions

Heat the canola oil in each of three sauté pans. Season, and sear the filets first, and let brown for 2 minutes. Season, and sear the chicken and the shrimp in the other 2 pans. Turn over the filets, and reduce the heat to medium. Cook until they have reached your desired temperature. Remove from heat, and let rest a couple of minutes.

When the chicken and shrimp are brown, turn them over, and sauté an additional 2 minutes or until done. Remove the chicken from the pan, and drain the fat. Add the 3 tablespoons of lemon juice to deglaze the chicken pan. Add the heavy cream, and bring to a boil for 5 minutes to reduce the sauce. Add the fresh basil, salt and pepper. Check the seasoning, and remove from heat.

Plating

Evenly divide the Whipped Yukon Potatoes over the 4 plates, and place in the center of each, creating a line approximately 6 " long. Place 1 filet, 2 pieces of chicken and 2 shrimp in a row atop the potatoes. Napé the cream sauce over the proteins, and lean 5 pieces of Grilled Asparagus against the proteins as shown on page 119.

Pan Seared Salmon
with Roasted Yukon Potatoes
and Cilantro-Lime Glaze

4 ea	8 oz salmon filets, skin removed
2 T	canola oil
TT	kosher salt
TT	black pepper, coarse grind
3 T	canola oil
6 oz	honey
2 T	butter, unsalted
1 T	lime juice
½ tsp	cilantro

Ratatouille

1 T	butter, unsalted
2 oz	zucchini, ¼" dice
2 oz	yellow squash, ¼" dice
2 oz	red onion, ¼" dice
2 oz	red peppers, ¼" dice
1 ea	sprig of fresh thyme, leaves only
TT	kosher salt
TT	black pepper, coarse grind

Roasted Potatoes

2 T	butter
1 lb	Yukon "c" potatoes, halved
TT	kosher salt
TT	black pepper, coarse grind
4 ea	lime wedges

Yield: 4 portions

Put the first oil on a large plate, and drag each salmon filet through the oil to coat both sides of each piece. Season each with salt and pepper. Get 2 large sauté pans smoking hot, and add the second portion of canola oil to each. Place 2 salmon filets in each pan with what was the skin side facing up. Allow to brown over high heat for approximately 2 minutes, and place in a 375-degree oven. Do not flip the salmon. Cook for approximately 5 minutes.

Ratatouille

Melt the butter in a medium-sized skillet. Add the onions, and sauté until translucent. Add the zucchini, yellow squash, red peppers, and thyme. Sauté until tender, stirring frequently. Season to taste with salt and pepper.

Roasted Potatoes

Melt the butter in a large skillet, and add the Yukon potato halves. Sauté over high heat for 2 to 3 minutes. Season with salt and pepper, and place the sauté pan in a 375-degree oven for 15 minutes. Remove from the oven, and, using a spatula, loosen the potatoes from the pan. Try to get the brown side up on some of the potatoes, and return the pan to the oven for an additional 15 minutes. Test to see if they are done by using a paring knife held between the thumb and the baby finger. Insert it into one of the larger potatoes, and if there is little resistance, they are done.

continues next page...

Plating

Divide the roasted potatoes onto the center of 4 plates. Divide the ratatouille onto the 4 plates, spooning it over the potatoes. Next, remove the salmon from the pan with a thin spatula, and turn the fish over onto the potatoes and ratatouille mixture, so that the crispy side is facing up. Add the honey and lime juice to the hot pan, and stir with a wooden spoon for 1 minute. Add the cilantro and the butter, remove from the heat, and stir until smooth. Pour evenly over the 4 plates. Serve with a lime wedge and chopped cilantro garnish.

Pan Seared Halibut with Dried Apricot Risotto

Once again we are mixing flavors, colors, and textures to create a meal that pleases the eye as well as the palate. The sweetness of the apricot risotto, combined with the salty flavor of the sweet potato chips, is a winner every time! Have the risotto started and close to finished when beginning to sear the halibut. Have the sweet potato chips already done as well.

1 T	canola oil
2 ea	7 oz. halibut filets, boneless and skinless
TT	kosher salt
TT	black pepper, coarse grind
12 oz	Dried Apricot Risotto (page 182)
4 oz	sweet potato chips (page 190)

Yield: 2 portions

Heat the oil in a medium-sized skillet until smoking hot. Season the halibut filets, and place them in the pan with what was the skin side facing up. Allow the halibut filets to brown until golden. Without turning the fish over, place the skillet in a 375-degree oven for approximately 5 minutes or until the fish is cooked through.

Plating

Place half of the risotto on each of the 2 plates. Next, using a thin spatula, place the halibut filets on top of the risotto, turning it over as you do so. This will give you the crispy side of the halibut facing up. Sprinkle half of the sweet potato chips on top of the halibut.

Side Dishes

I have tried to give you a fair amount of side dishes to choose from for making your main meals great.

Unfortunately, there isn't enough room in this book to cover all the side dishes I would have liked.

I did cover the basics though. You have a wonderful whipped potato recipe, a few variations of risotto, vegetables, and root vegetable chips, which make an awesome accompaniment to any meal or can be used as a snack by themselves.

Always take the same pride in preparing your side dishes as you do with the main courses. Remember, everything you serve will be eaten. It should all taste great!

Dried Apricot Risotto

The trick to a good risotto is stirring often until it is done and serving it immediately.

1 T	canola oil
2 T	shallots, minced
3 T	dried apricots, small dice
4 oz.	arborio rice
2 cups	Roasted Chicken Stock (page 143)
3 T	butter, unsalted
2 T	Romano cheese, grated
1/4 tsp	kosher salt
1/4 tsp	black pepper, coarse grind

Yield: 4 portions

In a 2-quart sauce pot, heat the canola oil over medium heat. Add the shallots, and cook until translucent, about 1 minute. Add the dried apricots and the rice, and continue to stir for about 1 minute. Add about 1/3 of the Roasted Chicken Stock, and bring to a boil while stirring. Reduce to a slow simmer. Keep an eye on the pot, and stir a little more often than occasionally. Once the stock has been absorbed by the rice, add another 1/3 of the stock. Continue to stir the rice occasionally, and add more stock as needed. The rice is done when it is "al dente" but not crunchy.

Once the rice is done, remove it from the stove, and stir in the butter and cheese. Season with salt and pepper. The risotto should run a bit when you put it on the plate and not be a blob.

Grilled Asparagus

2 qts	boiling water
½ tsp	kosher salt
20 stalks	large asparagus, stems peeled
1 T	canola oil
TT	kosher salt
TT	black pepper, coarse grind
1 T	butter, unsalted

Yield: 4 portions

Bring the water and salt to a boil. Add the asparagus, and boil for 2 minutes. Remove, and plunge the asparagus into ice water.

In a bowl, place the oil and a pinch of salt and pepper. Toss the asparagus in the oil so it becomes evenly coated with the oil and seasoning.

Put the asparagus on a hot grill, and cook for about 2 minutes.

Remove and serve.

Grilled Corn

There are many uses for Grilled Corn.

It can be used in fillings for raviolis; a recipe is included in this book.

It makes a great salsa, also included in this book. I like to add it as a garnish to salads of all kinds. The flavor it adds is spectacular! It can be used in a stuffing for meat, poultry, pork, and lamb. The uses are endless. If you were to add Roasted Chicken Stock, cream, blend, and then strain it, of course, the sauce would compliment dozens of dishes.

4 ea	ears of corn, shucked
1 T	vegetable oil
TT	kosher salt
TT	black pepper, coarse grind

Yield: Approximately 2 ½ cups

Lightly coat the ears of corn with oil and grill until the kernels are golden brown. When grilling, be sure to roll the ears across the grill to get evenly browned without being burned. Although a few dark kernels do add a nice charred flavor, be careful!

Once the corn is the desired color, place in a preheated 350-degree oven for approximately 5 minutes. Remove from the oven, and let cool.

Cut the kernels from the ear, and season with salt and pepper.

The ears add terrific flavor to soup stocks and sauces! Just simmer in the stock or sauce until the desired flavor is attained.

Grilled Corn Salsa

This is a great accompaniment to a variety of dishes. My favorite is to serve it with crab cakes and Pico di Gallo Mayo. It goes well with grilled white fish, such as grouper, snapper, and halibut. You can also use this in place of dressing on salads. It will add flavor without all the fat!

2 cups	Grilled Corn (page 184)
1 ea	jalapeño peppers
1 tsp	cilantro, chopped
¼ cup	red peppers, small dice
¼ cup	green peppers, small dice
¼ cup	red onion, small dice
1 T	lime juice
2 T	canola oil
2 T	rice wine vinegar or rice wine
TT	kosher salt
TT	black pepper, coarse grind

Yield: Approximately 3 cups

Place all the ingredients in a mixing bowl, and mix well. Check the seasoning. Allow to chill a few hours before serving so the flavors can blend. Remix and serve.

Grilled Corn and Black Bean Salsa

Follow the above recipe, and add 1 cup of cooked black beans, ¼ tsp of cayenne pepper, and ¼ tsp of ground cumin.

Marinated Cherry Tomatoes

16 each	cherry tomatoes
2 T	extra virgin olive oil
1/2 tsp	garlic, fresh chopped
pinch	kosher salt
pinch	black pepper, coarse grind
1/2 tsp	basil, fresh chopped

Yield: 4 portions

Mix together, and allow to marinate 4-6 hours.

Oven Roasted Tomatoes

When making your own Oven Roasted Tomatoes, you have the luxury of creating a product to be used in other recipes to fit your own personal taste. Follow my recipe the first time, and then, in the future, adjust the cooking time. Longer cooking time will result in a drier and somewhat sweeter tomato. Add more garlic if that is your desire. Add other herbs such as oregano, basil, marjoram, etc. You can increase the salt level, the olive oil level, you get the drift. Enjoy your creative side.

1/4 cup	extra virgin olive oil
1/2 tsp	garlic, chopped
1/4 tsp	sugar
1/2 tsp	kosher salt
1/4 tsp	black pepper, coarse grind
12 ea	plum tomatoes, cut in half, lengthwise, seeds removed

Yield: 24 halves

Heat the oil In a small sauté pan until hot. Remove the pan from the heat, and add the garlic. Stir the garlic until it turns white, about 30-45 seconds. Add the sugar, salt, and pepper.

Arrange the tomatoes on a parchment-lined cookie sheet, skin side down.

Brush the tomatoes with the olive oil mixture, and place in a 275-degree oven for 1 hour. Check the tomatoes. They should be fairly dry with the edges beginning to brown. You can keep them in the oven an additional 20 minutes if you desire.

Remove and let cool. These will keep in a refrigerator for up to 1 week.

Potato Galette

2 cups	shredded potatoes, no skins
½ tsp	kosher salt
½ tsp	black pepper, coarse grind
4 T	vegetable oil

Yield: 4 portions

Mix potatoes, salt and pepper in a mixing bowl. Divide into 4 even portions.

Heat 1 T of oil until it flows like water in an 8" sauté pan. Add 1 portion of the potatoes spread evenly in the pan, and press firmly using a small spatula. The galettes should be ½" thick. Cook until golden brown and flip. Cook until golden brown, remove from the pan, and place on a cookie sheet. Repeat this 3 more times. When potatoes are needed for your dish, heat in a 350-degree oven for 4 minutes.

Smoked Gouda Croutons

These croutons make any salad taste great. They are also good as an appetizer. They don't need anything to enhance their flavor, but as an appetizer, served with your favorite ranch dressing, they are fabulous!

20 ea	smoked gouda pieces, ¾" square, rind removed
¼ cup	all purpose flour
1 ea	egg
2 oz	cold water
1 cup	panko breadcrumbs
As needed	frying oil
TT	kosher salt

Yield: 20 croutons

Mix the egg and cold water in a small bowl to make an egg wash. Toss the gouda cubes in a separate bowl with the flour. Remove the gouda cubes from the bowl, and shake off the excess flour. Dip the cubes into the egg wash. Again, shake off the excess, and coat in the panko breadcrumbs. Fry in 350-degree oil until golden brown. Season with salt, and serve.

Roasted Cauliflower Purée

This is a nice side dish that we serve with our Pan Seared Scallop entrée. Once you have tried it, you will see there are many uses. Experiment!

1 ea	head of cauliflower, leaves removed
1 T	canola oil
TT	kosher salt
TT	black pepper, coarse grind
4 oz	heavy cream
3 T	butter
½ tsp	white truffle oil

Yield: 4 portions

Rub the head of cauliflower with the canola oil. Season with the salt and pepper, and bake in a 450-degree oven for 25 minutes, or until the outside of the cauliflower is golden brown. Remove from the oven, and chop it rough so that it will fit in your food processor.

While the cauliflower is baking, heat the cream, butter, and white truffle oil to a simmer. Put the chopped cauliflower in the food processor, and purée with the heated cream mixture. Purée until smooth, stopping the food processor periodically to scrape the sides. The purée should be thick, and there should be no lumps when done correctly. If it is too thick, add a little cream. Check the seasoning and adjust if necessary.

Root Vegetable Chips

Vegetable chips are a great way to garnish a main course. We use carrot, sweet potato, parsnips, and celery root. Purple potatoes, turnips, and most any other tuber can be used. A tuber is the fleshy root system of a plant. Plantains also make good chips if you are so inclined to expand your culinary repertoire!

The trick to creating good vegetable chips is to have the frying oil at the right temperature.

If the product to be fried has a high moisture content, I like to lower the oil temperature, and fry it for a little longer. A drier vegetable can be cooked at a higher temperature.

4 oz	sweet potatoes, sliced thin
4 oz	carrots, sliced thin on the bias, 2"–3" long
4 oz	turnips, sliced thin on the bias 2"–3" long
As needed	frying oil
As needed	kosher salt

Yield: Approximately 4 portions

Once you have sliced your vegetables, spread them out on a cookie sheet to separate each chip as best you can. Do not mix the vegetables, as they will have varying cooking times. Sprinkle the slices into a fryer that is at 325 degrees. Use a stainless steel spoon to separate the chips while cooking. Fry until the edges of the chips are golden brown. Remove from the oil, and place on paper towels to absorb any excess oil. Season with salt immediately.

The first time you do this you may remove the chips too early or too late. Practice makes perfect.

Don't give up. Once you have perfected this, they make a great snack or garnish. Enjoy!

Spiced Pecans

Spiced pecans make a great snack. They also give salads a nice texture and flavor. I like to add Spiced Pecans to a spinach stuffing for lamb or pork. Here is an easy recipe, so you can whip them up in no time at all.

2 T	unsalted butter
2 cups	pecan halves
1/3 cup	light brown sugar
¼ tsp	cayenne pepper
¼ tsp	ground cinnamon
¼ tsp	ground allspice
1 T	cold water

Yield: 2 cups

Melt the butter in a medium-sized sauté pan over medium-high heat. Add the pecan halves, and sauté until golden brown, about 3 minutes. Add the brown sugar, cayenne, cinnamon, and allspice. Stir until the pecans are evenly coated and the sugar has caramelized. This should only take 2 minutes or so. Remove from the heat, add the tablespoon of water, stir, and spread the pecans on a lightly-greased cookie sheet. Place in a 300-degree oven for 20 minutes. Let cool and eat!

Sun Dried Tomato Risotto

Do not be intimidated by making risotto. It is really an easy dish to prepare. Yes, you need to pay attention to what you are doing, but once you have made it correctly once, you'll be making it often. The trick to a good risotto is to keep stirring until it is done and to serve immediately.

I had a chef work for me once who was often heard to say, "Risotto waits for no man." He meant that once it is done correctly, it is ready to serve immediately.

Use arborio or carnaroli rice. They are short and plump, have a high starch content, and can absorb a lot of liquid.

Typically, rice is cooked with 2 parts water to 1 part rice. With risotto, plan on 3 parts stock to 1 part rice.

1 T	olive oil
2 T	shallots, minced
2 T	sun dried tomatoes, small dice
4 oz	arborio rice
2 cups	Roasted Chicken Stock, previously prepared (page 143)
3 T	butter, unsalted
2 T	romano cheese, grated
1/4 tsp	kosher salt
1/4 tsp	black pepper, coarse grind

Yield: 4 portions

In a 2-quart sauce pot, heat the olive oil over medium heat. Add the shallots, and cook until translucent, about 1 minute. Add the rice, and continue to stir for about 1 minute. Add about 1/3 of the Roasted Chicken Stock, and bring it to a boil while stirring. Reduce to a slow simmer. Keep an eye on the pot, and stir a little more often than occasionally. Once the stock has been absorbed by the rice, add another 1/3 of the stock and the sun dried tomatoes. Continue to stir the rice occasionally, and add more stock as needed. The rice is done when it is "al dente" but not crunchy.

Once the rice is done, remove it from the stove, and stir in the butter and cheese. Season with salt and pepper. The risotto should run a bit when you put it on the plate and not be a blob.

Butternut Risotto

Follow the recipe above substituting 1 cup of ½" diced butternut squash for the sun-dried tomatoes.

The squash should be blanched for 2 minutes in salted boiling water. Add the second 1/3 of Roasted Chicken Stock when cooking the risotto. Also, stir in 1 T of maple syrup with the first addition of Roasted Chicken Stock.

Lemon-Pepper Risotto

Again, follow the recipe above, and omit the sun dried tomatoes. Add 1 tsp of lemon zest and ½ tsp of black pepper at the beginning of the cooking process.

Whipped Yukon Potatoes

Ahhh, comfort food! Correctly made whipped potatoes make any dish great. The problem is we are taught to use milk instead of cream as a way to save money. Margarine is substituted for butter for health reasons, and seasoning is an after thought. Follow this recipe, and do not substitute any ingredients, and then enjoy the best potatoes you've ever made!

5 lbs	Yukon potatoes, peeled, quartered
As needed	water, cold
1 tsp	kosher salt
8 oz	butter, unsalted, melted
2 cups	heavy cream
1/2 tsp	black pepper, coarse grind
1 1/2 tsp	kosher salt

Yield: Approximately 15 portions

Place the peeled potatoes in an 8-quart stockpot, cover with cold water and salt. Bring to a boil, and cook until tender. This will take approximately 20 minutes after the water comes to a boil. A good way to test if the potatoes are ready is to poke them with a paring knife held between the baby finger and the thumb. You don't have as much strength when holding the knife this way, and you will be able to feel any resistance. The knife should slide in easily, but not too easy.

When the potatoes are cooked, remove them from the heat and strain out all the liquid. Place the potatoes on a cookie sheet and put in a 375-degree preheated oven for about 10 minutes to evaporate any excess moisture.

At this point, I like to run the potatoes through a food mill to remove all lumps. You don't need to do this, but, if you have a food mill, go ahead.

Place the butter, cream, salt, and pepper in the pot the potatoes were cooked in. Bring to a boil, and add the potatoes. Whip until fluffy. Do not over whip as this will create a gummy texture.

Yukon Potato Chips

At Keon's, we like to serve these potato chips with our Korean BBQ Pork appetizer. I like to snack on them every time I go through the kitchen. It drives my chefs crazy!

2 ea	Yukon gold potatoes, sliced thin on a mandolin
As needed	frying oil, hot
TT	kosher salt

Yield: 2-4 portions

Individually drop ¼ of the chips into oil that is 350 degrees. Stir them with a metal spoon to separate them from each other. Fry for 2 minutes or until golden brown.

Remove them from the oil, and place on a papyrus plate to absorb the extra oil. Season immediately with kosher salt. Cool and serve—or don't cool them, they're great hot out of the fryer!

Sweet Potato Chips

2 ea	sweet potatoes, peeled and sliced thin on a mandolin
As needed	frying oil, hot
TT	kosher salt

Yield: 2-4 portions

Individually drop ¼ of the chips into oil that is 350 degrees. Stir them with a metal spoon to separate them from each other. Fry for 2-4 minutes or until golden brown.

Remove them from the oil, and place on a papyrus plate to absorb the extra oil. Season immediately with kosher salt. Cool and serve—or don't cool them, they're great hot out of the fryer! Sweet potato chips will take longer to cook than the Yukon Potato Chips. Keep an eye on them.

    Keon's Kitchen – Secret Recipes from the Award-Winning Restaurant

Desserts

Desserts are usually a sweet dish made from fruit, ice cream, pastry, or cake served at the end of a meal.

The recipes that follow are easy to make and do not take much time to prepare.

Dessert has always been my favorite part of the meal. Who can resist something sweet?

Unfortunately, there was not enough room in the book to offer more recipes. But who knows? Maybe in the next book...

Blueberry Cobbler

Cobblers are some of my favorite desserts. The blueberries can be substituted for stone fruits such as peaches, apricots, nectarines, etc.

Apples always make good cobblers. Just substitute the blueberries with the desired fruit, and follow the directions exactly.

Biscuits

1 ¼ cups	all purpose flour
1/3 cup	sugar
1 ½ tsp	baking powder
½ tsp	salt
¼ tsp	ground nutmeg
¼ cup	butter, cold
½ cup	milk, cold
1 tsp	sugar, large granules (decorating sugar)

Fruit Mixture

¾ cup	sugar
2 T	all purpose flour
5 cups	blueberries, frozen
2 tsp	lemon peel, grated
1 T	lemon juice

Yield: Approximately 12 portions

Heat oven to 400 degrees. Grease a 9" x 13" glass casserole dish with butter or Pam non-stick spray.

In a medium-sized bowl, stir together 1 1/4 cups flour, 1/3 cup sugar, baking powder, salt and nutmeg. "Cut in" the butter using a fork or pastry cutter until the mixture looks like coarse crumbs. Stir in milk until just combined, set aside.

In a 2½-quart sauce pan, (preferably stainless steel) stir together ¾ cup sugar and 2 T of flour. Mix in the blueberries, lemon peel, and lemon juice. Heat to boiling over medium-high heat, stirring constantly. Pour into the baking dish.

Immediately spoon the biscuit dough onto the hot mixture. Sprinkle the decorating sugar crystals over the dough. Bake 25-35 minutes or until biscuits are golden brown. Cool at least 10 minutes before serving.

Chocolate Chip Bread Pudding

I love bread pudding! All bread puddings are basic custards. A basic custard is eggs, cream, and sugar. Flavorings vary from recipe to recipe.

The first 3 ingredients in this recipe constitute a basic custard recipe. You can add grape nuts, a variety of cereals, croissants, breads, and even fruits, like blueberries, to change it up a bit.

8 ea	eggs
8 oz	sugar
1 qt	light cream
2 T	vanilla extract
¼ tsp	kosher salt
6 cups	old bread, cut into 1"-2" pieces
12 oz	chocolate chips
3 T	sugar in the raw

Yield: 1 – 9" x 13" baking dish

In a medium-sized bowl, mix the eggs, sugar, cream, vanilla extract, and salt together.

Mix the bread and chocolate chips in a greased, 9"x 13" baking dish. Pour the egg mixture over the bread, and be sure the chocolate is evenly distributed.

Bake in a 325-degree oven for 25 minutes. Sprinkle the sugar in the raw over the entire pudding. Bake an additional 15 minutes. Check with a toothpick. If it comes out clean, the bread pudding is done. If there is a moist coating on the toothpick, put the pudding back in the oven for a few minutes, and check again.

Old Fashioned Bread Pudding

I love bread pudding! All bread puddings are basic custards. A basic custard is eggs, cream, and sugar. Flavorings vary from recipe to recipe.

The first 3 ingredients in this recipe are a basic custard recipe. You can add grape nuts, a variety of cereals, croissants, breads, and even fruits, like blueberries, to change it up a bit.

8 ea	eggs
8 oz	sugar
1 qt	light cream
3/4 cup	raisins
2 T	vanilla extract
1/4 tsp	kosher salt
12 slices	bread, white or wheat
1/4 cup	sugar in the raw

Yield: 1 – 9" x 13" baking dish

In a medium-sized bowl, mix the eggs, sugar, cream, raisins, vanilla extract, and salt together. Let sit in the refrigerator for 1-2 hours so the raisins can absorb some liquid.

Layer the bread in a greased 9" x 13" baking dish. Pour the egg mixture over the bread and be sure the raisins are evenly distributed.

Bake in a 325-degree oven for 25 minutes. Sprinkle the sugar in the raw over the entire pudding. Bake an additional 15 minutes. Check with a toothpick. If it comes out clean, the bread pudding is done. If there is a moist coating on the toothpick, put the pudding back in the oven for a few minutes, and check again.

Glossary

Bisque – A thick cream soup or purée of shellfish or vegetables.

Blanch – To par cook in boiling water. After blanching, it is recommended to shock the item in cold water to stop the cooking process. This will give vegetables a brilliant color.

Braise – A combination of dry and moist heat. Dry heat being the oven and moist heat being the liquid the protein is cooked in. This is a common way to tenderize tough meats. Braising is done in a covered pot that has been brought to a boil and placed in a low heat oven for a period of time.

Brine – To immerse, preserve, or pickle in salt water.

Caramelize – To heat sugar until it melts and reaches a brown color. To caramelize vegetables or proteins is to cook in a very hot pan to brown the natural sugars of the product.

Chiffonade – An 1/8"x 2" cut of a soft herb, lettuce, or vegetable. Basil chiffonade makes a great garnish while adding flavor.

Chutney – A highly seasoned relish made from fruits, sugar, vinegar, and spices. Its origin is India.

Confit – This is a process of preserving meat, typically duck, goose, or pork, by curing with salt and then poaching it in its own fat. Yummy!

Curing – To preserve meat by salting, smoking, or aging.

Deglaze – To add cold liquid to a hot pan. This is to loosen the caramelized proteins from the pan. These drippings are a wonderful beginning to many sauces.

Demi Glace – A reduced veal stock.

Egg Wash – A mixture of equal parts egg and water, used for sealing pastries and pastas; also used for giving baked products a nice shine.

Emulsified – A dressing or sauce in which liquid has been suspended in fat or oil. Mayonnaise is an emulsified dressing.

EVOO – An extra virgin olive oil. This is the first, cold press of the olives. EVOO is best used for dressings and when finishing a sauce or dish. It is not recommended for sautéing. It has a low smoking point and gives a bitter flavor to the food it is sautéed with.

Extra Heavy Mayonnaise – This can be found in your local supermarket. The label will indicate if it is extra heavy. If you cannot find extra heavy, use a brand name.

Frenched – This is when the fat and sinew have been totally removed from between the bones of veal, pork, or lamb chops.

Galette – A potato dish where the potato is shredded and seared in a pan until golden brown. It is similar to a round hash brown.

Haricots Vert – These are French-style green beans, usually consistent in size and a bit sweeter than string beans.

Julienne – This is a knife-cut of vegetable. It should measure 1/8"x 1/8" x 2-2 ½".

Marinade – A combination of acid, oil, and seasonings used to flavor and tenderize meats, fish, and poultry.

Marinate – To soak or steep in a marinade.

Monte au Beurre – To finish with butter. This is to take cold butter and whisk it into a simmering sauce. This will thicken the sauce, and also it adds a sheen to it.

Nape' – To sauce a dish over the top. When napéing, the sauce should be fairly thick. Classically speaking, it should coat the back of a wooden spoon. An example of napéing can be seen in the photo of the Surf, Surf, and Turf on page 115.

Panko Breadcrumbs – Panko is a variety of breadcrumb from Japanese and French cuisine used to create a crunchy coating for fried foods. Panko is made from bread without crusts, and it has a crisper, airier texture than most types of breading found in Western cuisine.

Pan Sear – This is the same as sautéing. Remember, use a very hot pan, then add oil. Once the oil flows like water, you are ready to add your product.

Par Cook – To cook part-way.

Render – To reduce, convert, or melt down fat by heating.

Rest/Resting – This is done before and after cooking meats. Allowing a steak to rest at room temperature for 30 minutes prior to cooking will give you a more tender steak. Allowing it to rest after it is cooked for 5-10 minutes will give the meat time to retain its natural juices. Not allowing a steak to rest after cooking will result in the juices leaking all over your plate when you cut into the steak.

Rondo – A wide cooking vessel that tends to be wider than it is high, giving more surface area for cooking.

Sabayon – A sauce or dessert composed of eggs, white wine, sugar, and flavorings.

Sauté – To jump in the pan. In order to properly sauté, one must have a very hot pan. The pan should be heated prior to adding oil.

Simmer – To cook in liquid where the bubbles are just breaking the surface.

Slurry – A mixture of equal parts of corn starch and cold water. When mixed smooth, it is used for thickening sauces by whisking it into the simmering liquid. A flour slurry can also be used.

Stock – A liquid in which bones, meats and vegetables are simmered.

Sweat – To sauté vegetables over a medium heat to open the pores and extract the most flavor.

TT – "To Taste" or to season to taste. This means to add salt and pepper, taste it, and add more if necessary. Remember, even if you are not fond of salt, but you want to serve great food, you still need to season with salt and pepper so your guests are not tasting bland food.

Translucent – This is when sautéing onions over high heat—they will clear before browning. This is translucent.

Uncooked Roux – This is called "beurre manie" in French. It is equal parts flour and softened butter blended together. It is whisked into a simmering sauce to thicken it. 4 oz of uncooked roux will thicken 1 qt of liquid.